FOR THE UNITY OF ALL

For the Unity of All

Contributions to the Theological Dialogue
between East and West

John Panteleimon Manoussakis

Foreword by
His All-Holiness the Ecumenical Patriarch Bartholomew I

CASCADE *Books* • Eugene, Oregon

FOR THE UNITY OF ALL
Contributions to the Theological Dialogue between East and West

Copyright © 2015 John Panteleimon Manoussakis. All rights reserved. Except for brief quotations in critical publications or reviews, no part of this book may be reproduced in any manner without prior written permission from the publisher. Write: Permissions, Wipf and Stock Publishers, 199 W. 8th Ave., Suite 3, Eugene, OR 97401.

Cascade Books
An Imprint of Wipf and Stock Publishers
199 W. 8th Ave., Suite 3
Eugene, OR 97401

www.wipfandstock.com

ISBN 13: 978-1-4982-0042-4

Cataloging-in-Publication data:

Manoussakis, John Panteleimon

    For the unity of all : contributions to the theological dialogue between east and west / John Panteleimon Manoussakis ; foreword by Patriarch Bartholomew.

    xx + 102 p. ; 23 cm. —Includes bibliographical references and index.

    ISBN 13: 978-1-4982-0042-4

    1. Orthodox Eastern Church—Relations—Catholic Church. 2. Orthodox Eastern Church—Doctrines. 3. Catholic Church—Doctrines. 4. Christian union—Orthodox Eastern Church. 6. Christian union—Catholic Church. I. Bartholomew I, Ecumenical Patriarch of Constantinople, 1940–. II. Title.

BX324.3 .M36 2015

Manufactured in the U.S.A.

For His Holiness

Pope Francis

and

His All-Holiness

The Ecumenical Patriarch Bartholomew I

On the Fiftieth Anniversary of the Historic Encounter between Their Predecessors

Pope Paul VI and Patriarch Athenagoras

1964–2014

Ut unum sint!

Contents

Foreword by His All-Holiness the Ecumenical Patriarch Bartholomew I | ix
Acknowledgments | xi
Introduction | xiii

Part One: Revisiting Theological Differences | 1

    ONE Mary's Exception | 5

    Two The Procession of the Holy Spirit | 15

    THREE The Petrine Primacy | 21

  ADDENDUM TO PART ONE: *Unitatis Rediniegratio* Fifty Years Later | 44

Part Two: Differences in Theological Style Reconciled

    FOUR Created and Uncreated Light:
              Augustinian and Palamite Approaches | 51

    FIVE Will and Grace: Augustinian and Maximian Approaches | 69

Bibliography | 93
Index | 101

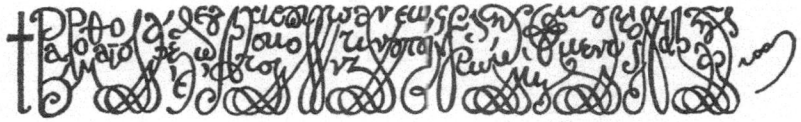

Foreword

IT IS WITH JOY that we welcome and recommend *For the Unity of All*, by the Reverend Dr. John Panteleimon Manoussakis.

For several decades now, especially since the historical meeting in January 1964 of our predecessor, the late Ecumenical Patriarch Athenagoras, with the late Pope Paul VI in Jerusalem, the Orthodox Church and the Roman Catholic Church have made significant progress toward reconciliation as obedience to our Lord's prayer and commandment "that His disciples may be one" (John 17:21), as well as toward the realization of their identity as "sister churches."

What occurred in 1964 was little noticed at the time. Nevertheless, it was an extraordinary departure from the inexcusably cold and hitherto nonexistent relations between our two churches over many centuries. It led to the mutual lifting of the anathemas only a year later, the exchange of visitations at the respective patronal feasts, and ultimately the theological dialogue between our two churches. Thus, the "dialogue of love" gradually prompted and progressed into the "dialogue of truth."

One of the most significant issues embraced in recent years by the joint international commission for this dialogue has been the difference in methodological and theological approaches to primacy in the Church. This book contributes to the ongoing discussion of this crucial topic.

At the Ecumenical Patriarchate, Theophany 2014

Your fervent supplicant before God,

✠ BARTHOLOMEW
Archbishop of Constantinople-New Rome
and Ecumenical Patriarch

Acknowledgments

I AM THANKFUL TO His Eminence Metropolitan John of Pergamon (Zizioulas), who, in his capacity as the co-president, allowed me to attend the ninth plenary session of the Joint International Commission on the Theological Dialogue between the Roman Catholic Church and the Orthodox Church in Belgrade, an experience that gave me the initial inspiration for this book; the influence of his theological work can be felt in every page of the present work.

I am also thankful to His Eminence Metropolitan Methodios of Boston, in whose Metropolis I have the privilege to serve and whose commitment on the ecumenical dialogue has been a personal example.

I am grateful to His Excellence Archbishop of Lecce Domenico Umberto D'Ambrosio for his kind invitation to give a lecture in Lecce in honor of the Ecumenical Patriarch's twentieth anniversary from his election to the apostolic throne of St. Andrew. Most of the material for the first part of this book originated as part of that lecture. I am thankful to Dr. Massimo Vergari (of the Office of Ecumenical Relations of the Archdiocese of Lecce) and to Mrs. Isabella Bernardini D'Arnesano and to Mr. Awdie Coppola for facilitating that visit and providing me with unforgettable hospitality. Thanks are also due to Prof. Aristotle Papanikolaou for inviting me to give a paper at the conference "Orthodox Constructions of the West" at Fordham University. An earlier version of the discussion on primacy was first presented there and it was subsequently included in the proceedings of that conference.

I am also thankful to Bishop Maxim (Vasiljević) for his kind invitation to participate in the international conference on St. Maximus the Confessor in Belgrade, Serbia, in October 2012. The last chapter of the present book originated in that conference presentation.

Acknowledgments

The manuscript of this book was substantially improved by the corrections and comments of Fr. Mark Patrick Hederman, Abbot of Glenstal Abbey; Prof. Richard Kearney of Boston College; and two of my former students at the College of Holy Cross, Thomas Arralde (now brother Ambrose, OP) and Nicholas Powers. I am thankful to all of them for their willingness to read this work. I am also grateful for the support of my colleagues at the College of Holy Cross, in particular Fr. John Gavin, SJ.

I would also like to fulfill a promise and an obligation by thanking Dr. Artur Sebastian Rosman for a wise recommendation at a moment of despair. Finally, I am deeply grateful to my editors at Wipf and Stock, Dr. Charlie Collier and Mr. Jacob Martin, whose tremendous efficiency made the publication of this book so much more pleasurable. As always, I thank Dr. George Pelayo for his friendship and his unfailing support of my work.

Introduction

For the peace of the whole world, for the stability of the holy churches of God, and for the unity of all, let us pray to the Lord.

So reads the third petition of the great collect (ἡ μεγάλη συναπτή) with which every liturgical service in the Orthodox Church begins. In repeating these words the praying church echoes the prayer of its Lord, in which, we could say, the Church finds the beginnings and summation of its own liturgical life: "My prayer is not for them alone. I pray also for those who will believe in me through their message, *that all of them may be one*, Father, just as you are in me and I am in you. May they also be in us so that the world may believe that you have sent me" (John 17:20–21). The petition also recapitulates the early church's understanding of unity as, at once, a sign and a promise given to the Church. Thus St. Paul writes in the Epistle to the Ephesians:

> As a prisoner for the Lord, then, I urge you to live a life worthy of the calling you have received. Be completely humble and gentle; be patient, bearing with one another in love. Make every effort to keep the unity of the Spirit through the bond of peace. There is one body and one Spirit, just as you were called to one hope when you were called; *one Lord, one faith, one baptism; one God and Father of all, who is over all and through all and in all*. (Eph 4:1–6)

The very structure of the Church with its various ministries (a theme which will occupy our discussion in this book at some length by means of the dispute over Petrine ministry) reflects and safeguards the mystery of this mystical "unity of all":

Introduction

> So Christ himself gave the apostles, the prophets, the evangelists, the pastors and teachers, to equip his people for works of service, so that the body of Christ may be built up *until we all reach unity* in the faith and in the knowledge of the Son of God and become mature, attaining to the whole measure of the fullness of Christ. (Eph 4:11–13)

It seemed thus quite appropriate that the present essay in ecumenical theology[1] be named after so important and ancient a prayer: "for the unity of all."

The "cause" of the ecumenical dialogue between the Catholic and the Orthodox Church became a concern of mine a long time before I had any academic engagement with theology: it imposed itself on me as a problem in the days of my junior seminary in Athens, in the all too urgent form of my young classmates' hostility toward all things Latin. The first forms of this work, therefore, should be traced back to the debates that kept a number of young Orthodox seminarians up late at night, when the risk of being branded a sympathizer of the pope was much greater than the punishments we would have suffered had our schoolmaster found us out of our beds long after the lights had gone out.

It would have been difficult to imagine then that, only some years later, I should be given the opportunity to participate in the deliberations of a plenary meeting of the highest consultation on the theological dialogue between the two churches. I was afforded exactly that experience in September 2005, at the meeting of the Joint International Commission of the Theological Dialogue between the Orthodox Church and the Roman Catholic Church in Belgrade, Serbia. Other occasions of a similar nature were to follow: academic conferences and invited lectures that touched, one way or another, on the relations between the two churches.[2] Meanwhile, I had entered the

---

1. I borrow the term from Fr. Taft's recent exhortation to engage "an ecumenical scholarship and theology" (Taft, "Perceptions and Realities in Orthodox-Catholic Relations Today"). What such an ecumenical theology might look like is detailed as "a new and specifically Christian way of studying Christian tradition in order to reconcile and unite, rather than to confute and dominate. Its deliberate intention is to emphasize the common tradition underlying our differences, which though real, are usually the accidental product of history, culture, and language, rather than essential differences in the doctrine of faith" (38).

2. This book finds a distant origin in three such events: the first was a presentation on a panel of the American Academy of Religion's annual meeting in Washington DC, in 2006 that appeared subsequently in *Modern Theology* (26 [2010] 79–92) under the title "Theophany and Indication: Reconciling Augustinian and Palamite Aesthetics." The second was the conference "Orthodox Constructions of the West," organized in 2010 by

INTRODUCTION

monastic life and was ordained into the priesthood. Along with my ecclesiastical profession came the engagements of my professional life as an academic, teaching and writing at times on theological philosophy and at other, more daring moments on philosophical theology. The two occupations were never better harmonized than when I had to call on philosophy's resources in order to articulate or explain—I do not dare say "solve"—one of the problems which the futile polemics between the two churches passed down to us as our onerous inheritance. I am aware that, in doing so, I was humbly following, as a latecomer, a long line of tradition that goes back to the great synthesis of Athens with Jerusalem that took place during the Middle Ages, and extends as far back as St. Augustine, the Cappadocian Fathers, and the early Apologists. For philosophy has always played and continues to play an irreplaceable role in the articulation of the faith, as Joseph Ratzinger (now Pope Emeritus Benedict XVI) states quite unambiguously:

> As a theologian, I do not regard philosophy as being, ultimately, a study which we pursue for philosophy's sake. And yet how the very case at hand demonstrates that the integrity of faith depends on rigor of philosophical thinking, such that careful philosophizing is an irreplaceable part of genuine theological work.[3]

The tradition of employing philosophy's resourcefulness, theology's *ancilla* of old, in cultivating an ecumenical theology was not entirely lost in the times of modernity. The pioneer in what might be called "an ecumenical theology" was the great Renaissance philosopher and polymath Nicholas of Cusa, whose participation in two equally unsuccessful councils, Basel and Ferrara, provided him with the opportunity of some remarkable theological contributions.[4] Then there is also the example of Leibniz's

---

Profs. Aristotle Papanikolaou and George Demacopoulos at Fordham University. The third was a lecture given in December 2011 on the invitation of the Catholic Archdiocese of Lecce in honor of the twentieth anniversary of Patriarch Bartholomew's election to the throne of Constantinople. I am deeply thankful for these opportunities.

3. Ratzinger, *Eschatology*, 269.

4. These two councils could be considered a single one, as it was convoked by Pope Martin V in Basel, but it was later transferred to Ferrara (and then transferred once more to Florence) by Pope Eugene IV with the different purpose now of reuniting Eastern and Western Christendom. Nevertheless, a small group of dissident participants remained in Basel and continued with the council's deliberations on conciliarity and primacy. One cannot resist thinking of the similarities that that period of time bears to the present state of the ecumenical dialogue. The council at Ferrara-Florence effected a short-lived union with the East and it was recognized by the Catholic Church as its seventeenth Ecumenical Council. On the importance of that council on Cusanus's philosophical formation,

missions, officially entrusted on him, in facilitating the theological dialogue between the Catholic and the Protestant churches in the late seventeenth century. Even though the desired outcome of reunion was not one of the fruits of his labors, his efforts have given us some remarkable works, such as his *Dissertation on Predestination and Grace*.[5]

The book at hand provides its reader with two such examples: each of the two chapters of Part Two draws from contemporary philosophy and especially phenomenology, in an attempt to revisit some theological issues that have become points of contention between East and West.

The first of these chapters has to do with the (possibility of the) experience of God and the nature of such an experience. As a point of departure for that investigation serves the old debate on the hermeneutic of the Old Testament theophanies: how does God appear to Moses and Elijah and, for the Christian exegete, who—that is, which of the three persons of the Holy Trinity—appears? Two different answers have been given to these questions, behind which the alleged *difference* between Eastern and Western theology became exemplified and crystalized. On behalf of the latter spoke St. Augustine; in defense of the former wrote a late Byzantine theologian, St. Gregory Palamas. Our chapter reads the two fathers closely and with respect to their theological and historical idiosyncrasies, while it seeks to discover the common ground not only between Augustinian and Palamite theological aesthetics but, by extension, between two distinct—and for some antithetical—theological styles represented by these two theologians.

The second chapter ventures a similar attempt, but this time with respect to the relationship between the human will and the divine grace. On this score, too, some have seen East and West as standing on opposite sides, or at least as approaching this issue with different sensitivities, indicative, as they believe, of a different mindset that characterizes each church in opposition to the other. In this chapter we turn again to St. Augustine, not only because he is the father of the philosophical problem of the will as well as the doctor of grace, but because he is invariably seen by anti-Western authors as the instigator of every evil that befell the West—from the Great Schism to the Reformation and the Enlightenment and beyond.[6]

see Bond, "From Constantinople to 'Learned Ignorance.'"

5. For more on Leibniz's contribution to the ecumenical dialogue of his times, see Michael J. Murray's introduction to the English translation of this work: Murray, "Introduction."

6. Two recent volumes have contributed greatly to the appreciation of St. Augustine's position in Eastern Orthodox theology: Demacopoulos and Papanikolaou, *Orthodox*

Introduction

In both of these chapters, I have tried to demonstrate how theology can be done irenically and what the contribution of philosophy, especially contemporary continental philosophy, might be toward such reconciliatory theology. To this point, it is not without importance that both chapters find their resolution by appealing to and concluding with a treatment of eschatology. I have chosen to take St. Augustine as my common reference in both of these chapters, reading him in conjunction with two great Fathers that the Eastern Church has taken as defining its theological ethos, namely, St. Gregory Palamas, archbishop of Thessalonica (1296–1359) in chapter 4, and St. Maximus the Confessor (seventh century) in the fifth chapter.

Important as they may be, the theological subtleties treated in these two chapters are unlikely to be cited as the reasons over which the two churches separated from each other and are still kept apart. Thus, and because no book like this one would have been complete without a discussion of some of the more familiar themes of the theological divide, I have dedicated a substantial effort in Part One of this book to revisiting the questions of the Virgin Mary's immaculate conception, the Holy Spirit's procession (*filioque*), and the pope's Petrine ministry. Among these three topics, it is the last one that carries the greatest weight—as the other two are ultimately contested on procedural grounds, that is, on the pope's authority to define doctrine. Philosophy has played a significant role in the investigation of these three questions as well, although in subtler ways, perhaps, than in Part Two. Nevertheless, we believe that our discussion has opened some new windows that may bring a fresher air, if not a brighter light, to these old debates.

My approach in methodology was informed by the consideration that I write for the Catholic as well as the Orthodox reader, addressing their respective feelings of mistrust toward each other and taking into account the theological argumentation that they have advanced against each other over the past centuries. I write for the Catholic or Orthodox reader who would like to hear something different than precisely such an age-old argument. Finally, I write with the same passion for these issues that kept me up late at night in my junior seminary, believing that the Orthodox Church cannot be kept captive by its own past, ruminating the same line of arguments that first saw the light when Constantinople was still the Queen City of an empire. Thankfully, history did not end in 1453.

Readings of Augustine, and Plested, *Orthodox Readings of Aquinas*. Even though for Plested's monograph it is Aquinas's reception that is the central point, nevertheless, the Orthodox views on Augustine form a substantial part of his narrative.

Introduction

I have appealed to Catholic authorities when writing in support of what might be considered an Orthodox position, and I have invoked the testimony of the Greek Fathers and of the Orthodox liturgical life when defending what might look like a Catholic position. Yet, I have resisted treating this or that position as *a priori* Catholic or Orthodox, Eastern or Western, in fear of endlessly perpetuating a largely artificial opposition. The subtitle "Contributions to the Theological Dialogue" is appended to this book, and it is as such that my work will be received, I hope, becoming at the same time an invitation for others to join and further this dialogue.

This dialogue is not, in the words of Pope Francis and Patriarch Bartholomew,

> A mere theoretical exercise, but an exercise in truth and love that demands an ever deeper knowledge of each other's traditions in order to understand them and to learn from them. Thus we affirm once again that the theological dialogue does not seek a theological lowest common denominator on which to reach a compromise, but is rather about deepening one's grasp of the whole truth that Christ has given to his Church, a truth that we never cease to understand better as we follow the Holy Spirit's promptings. Hence, we affirm together that our faithfulness to the Lord demands fraternal encounter and true dialogue. Such a common pursuit does not lead us away from the truth; rather, through an exchange of gifts, through the guidance of the Holy Spirit, it will lead us into all truth (cf. Jn 16:13).[7]

This year marks the eve of the fiftieth anniversary of the first historic encounter in 1964 between the prelates of the two churches, Pope Paul VI and Ecumenical Patriarch Athenagoras, on the Mount of Olives—the precise place where, according to the Gospel of John, our Lord had uttered on the night before his Passion the petition "that they may all be one." It is difficult for us who measure time by the years of our lives to realize that fifty years measured against the Church's long history translate to a very brief span of time. In other words, it is still too early to fully assess the aftermath of that historic meeting. Yet, we have every reason to hope that it will not fail Christ's prayer.[8]

Without that inspired initiative of pope and patriarch who, guided by their fraternal love, left behind them the bitter animosity of centuries and embraced each other, a book such as this not only would have been

---

7. Bartholomew and Francis, Joint Declaration (Jerusalem, May 25, 2014).

8. On the historical and theological importance of this anniversary, see John Chryssavgis's commemorative volume, *Dialogue of Love*.

INTRODUCTION

impossible but also futile. It is therefore to their successors, Pope Francis and Ecumenical Patriarch Bartholomew, that the present volume is humbly and with great gratitude dedicated.

At the College of Holy Cross
On the Feast of St. John the Confessor, 2014

PART ONE

Revisiting Theological Differences

THE CATEGORIES "EAST" AND "West," when used in the context of church history, are not merely geographical demarcations, as if anything on the right of the Adriatic Sea was Eastern and everything on the left Western. Perhaps there was a time when those demarcations applied to a specific geography of what was known at the time as the *Oekoumene*; today, however, when there are Eastern churches and faithful in the West and Western churches in what can be called the East—even as far as the Far East—the terms *Eastern* and *Western* in ecclesiastical parlance mean simply a difference in *ethos*, in *liturgy*, and in *tradition*. Nor ought they to denote two different churches, for the "Western" church—if we allow for a moment this term to signify the Catholic Church—not only incorporates in its body *Eastern* churches, in the double sense of those churches that originated and flourished in the East (e.g., the Middle East) and of Eastern-rite communions, but also contains in her a number of "Eastern" characteristics in terms of the three parameters named above, namely, in ethos, liturgy, and tradition. The same can be said about the Orthodox Church—if we take her as an example of an "Eastern" Church. *Eastern* and *Western* are therefore nothing more than *terms of convenience* denoting the provenance of an idea or a practice, which could be applied to either of the two churches that progressively fell apart after the so-called Great Schism. It is only in this sense that they are employed here. Anything more would amount to "mak[ing] of an accident of geography a theological divide that simply is not there," to use the words of a Byzantine theologian who writes at the peak of anti-Western polemics.[1] "This absurd conflation of geography and

---

1. Demetrios Kydones, quoted in Plested, *Orthodox Readings of Aquinas*, 69.

Part One—Revisiting Theological Differences

theology," he continues, "represents a manifest betrayal of the truth, truth being the property neither of Asia nor of Europe."[2]

Furthermore, history challenges our view of a complete and immediate separation between East and West as some have often imagined it. The progress of alienation between the two churches was a slow and heterogeneous one—it did not take place in the same way, at the same time, and everywhere. As we would be right in saying that that progress of alienation began prior to the customary date of 1054, so it would be right to say that the union and communion between the two churches continued long after that date.[3] Like the terms *Eastern* and *Western*, historical dates and events become fixed only for the sake of our convenience. Be that as it may, our concerns here are not to engage in a lesson in either history or geography.

Rather, our goal is to offer some theological reflections on the issues that, for some time now, have been cited and presented as the grounds on which the separation of the two churches can be explained and, for some, even justified. By reflecting on these issues briefly, I hope to show whether they are real differences or only apparent ones—whether, that is, we can talk of different theologies or rather of *differences in theological styles*, and whether we may, by the support of the sustainer of the Church's unity, the Paraclete, and by the fervent intercessions of our common Mother, the Virgin Mary, if not overcome them, then at least explain them to each other.

I have selected three such topics of contention: one more liturgical, pertaining to the feast of the conception of the Virgin Mary; one more properly theological, concerning the procession of the Holy Spirit; and one ecclesiological, regarding the primacy of the pope. By categorizing or classifying each of these issues to a particular branch of the Church's

---

2. Ibid.

3. Fr. Andrew Louth, writing on the "Great Schism," observes that "the anathemas exchanged" in 1054 "were personal. Neither side claimed that the two halves of Christendom were in schism." And he continues that the Synod of Constantinople in 1089, under Patriarch Nicholas, "could find no evidence for a formal schism between East and West." Louth, *Greek East and Latin West*, 316–17. Indeed, even if one were to speak of a schism taking place in 1054 that would have involved at most the local churches of Rome and Constantinople, the remaining of the ancient patriarchates (Alexandria, Antioch, Jerusalem) did not became involved in the theological debate with Rome until much later, and they neither formally excommunicated the Roman See nor were excommunicated by it. Thus, historically, the so-called Great Schism remains nothing more than a conflict between two Sees of the same church and as such was repaired by the mutual annulment of the anathemas in 1965. See also Oeldemann, *Orthodoxe Kirchen im Ökumenischen Dialog*, 58.

Part One—Revisiting Theological Differences

life—liturgy, theology, ecclesiology—I do not mean to cancel out the understanding of the inseparability and unity of theology with liturgy, of liturgy with ecclesiology, and so on. In the life of the Church everything is an integral part of the whole and pertains to the whole; the Church is *one*—in this sense above all—as her Lord is one, and her faith is one. The issues that I have expressly named here, then, are each and all of them aspects of the Church's one faith.

One

Mary's Exception

LET ME BEGIN WITH the doctrine of the Virgin Mary's sanctification at conception. Devotion to the Virgin Mary is one of the profoundest common grounds between the Catholics and the Orthodox—in her we already recognize the reality of our unity, a unity of hearts, as well as the promise of our complete and perfect communion. It is, therefore, most unfortunate that the old polemics between the two churches should involve the most blessed person of the Mother of God. Some Orthodox theologians complain that the proclamation of the immaculate conception as a doctrine was a later addition in the history of dogma and, most importantly, a unilateral one.[1] In this, they are right. Nevertheless, such complaints lead us away from the real issue at hand to an unprofitable discussion on the history of doctrine. The theological question at hand is the following: *Is the Virgin Mary without sin or not?* The doctrine that proclaims that the Mother of God was sanctified at her conception comes to declare simply what every Christian, Orthodox or Catholic, has always believed about the person of the Theotokos, namely, that in her we find the most perfect human being—better yet, in her we see the true nature of a human person, a nature unafflicted by any sin, including the original sin. Some Orthodox

---

1. Even that complaint, though, is not entirely justifiable, as in pronouncing the doctrine of the immaculate conception as dogma the pope was relying on a tradition that was as much, if not more, Eastern (as I hope my analysis here will show) as it was Western. Thus, it could be said that the pope, in his capacity as the *primus* of the universal church (of which more below), was at that instance representing the Eastern churches as well. On the Eastern character of the doctrine of the immaculate conception, see Kappes, *The Immaculate Conception*.

theologians, under the influence of Protestant apologetics, have come to believe—and so they accuse the Catholics—that the doctrine of the immaculate conception makes the Virgin Mary *more* than a human being, that is, equal to the Son of God, and thus something like a Christian version of an ancient female deity, the *Magna Mater* of old. Such allegations betray the theological misunderstanding of those who formulate them and of those who repeat them. We ask: is sin natural for humans? Is humanity's original state, as it was intended by its creator, that which we know after the fall? If we answer these questions in the affirmative then everything is lost: not only have we condemned humanity to sin, but we render divine grace, repentance, forgiveness, and salvation not only superfluous but monstrous. For if sin is natural and part of our nature, that is, part and parcel of being human, then our salvation implies nothing less than the undoing of our humanity, the abuse of humanity into becoming something else, something that we not only are not but also cannot be: sinless.

On the contrary, the person of the Theotokos, affirmed as free from every sin, becomes an affirmation of humanity's original capacity to be without sin, or at least it assures us that we *could have been* without sin; it reveals to us that sin, contrary to our experience, is not necessary. It is this and nothing more that the doctrine of the immaculate conception declares. And it declares it in unity and harmony with the other great Marian feast, that of the Dormition or the Assumption of the Virgin Mary. How to explain what Christians have celebrated since at least the fifth century, that is, that Mary, even though she dies, is not dead; that her body does not see corruption but, together with her soul, experiences already the eschatological blessedness?[2] How to explain all this without recourse to the exceptional and singular grace that the Virgin Mary received as the Mother of God? In the feast of the Dormition—perhaps the most popular feast in the hearts of the Orthodox—we find the key to how the Orthodox could accept doctrinally what they already confess liturgically,[3] namely, the sinless nature of the Mother of God.

---

2. On the history of the feast of the Dormition or Assumption in the Eastern Church, see Brian Daley's introduction to *On the Dormition of Mary*. See also Pelikan, *Mary Through the Centuries*, in particular 201–13.

3. There are countless examples from the *lex orandi* of the Orthodox Church according to which the Virgin Mary is addressed as "immaculate" (ἄσπιλος)—most commonly the prayer that concludes the Small Compline—and ἄμωμος (see the hymnology of Orthros of the feast of the Dormition). For a complete study of the Marian feast according to the Eastern liturgy, see Kimball, *Liturgical Illuminations*.

Mary's Exception

Even the most polemical among the Orthodox do not, and indeed would not, contest the exceptional sanctity of the Virgin Mary—her most often used appellation as Παναγία (the most holy) suggests that much.[4] In the doctrine of the immaculate conception it is not the adjective "immaculate" that troubles the Orthodox, for such they would eventually acknowledge her, but rather the assertion that the immaculate status in question was enjoyed by the Virgin Mary already by the moment of her conception. The debate, therefore, between contemporary Orthodox theology and Catholic doctrine is not about the *what*, but only about the *when*. Both traditions would agree that she whom the archangel greeted with the words "full of grace" (κεχαριτωμένη, *gratia plena*) was indeed so and thus without sin. The difference, if any, comes down to the rather "scholastic" task of deciding the exact time at which such a designation takes effect.

Three crucial moments in the life of the Virgin Mary have been suggested as that time: *a*) as late as at the crucifixion of Christ, *b*) at the annunciation, and *c*) as early as at her own conception. In explaining Simeon's prophecy to Mary (Luke 2:35), Origen understands that the sword that pierced her soul was the scandal of seeing her son, whom she also knew as her God, dying on the cross:

> Why do we think that the mother of the Lord was immune from scandal when the apostles were scandalized? If she did not suffer scandal at the Lord's Passion, then Jesus did not die for her sins. But, "if all have sinned and lacked God's glory, but are justified by his grace and are redeemed" [Rom 3:23], then Mary too was scandalized at that time.[5]

For Origen, then, the event that causes Mary's sanctification, namely, Christ's sacrifice on the cross, coincides with or is followed closely by its effect. The argument here follows rather slavishly the logic of efficient causality. The redemptive work of the Savior, Origen seems to argue, was not completed until the moment of his passion; therefore, the effects of that redemption could not have been felt prior to that event. This logic makes no exception for the one person who has always been regarded by the Church as exceptional. There is little wonder, then, why Origen's argument—so rationalistic and, therefore, so Greek in its provenance—finds no followers

---

4. For a survey of the various Orthodox positions on this subject, from the Patristic era to the present, see Spourlakou-Eutychiadou, "The Most Holy Theotokos as a Model of Christian Sanctity."

5. Origen, *Homilies on Luke*, 73.

Part One—Revisiting Theological Differences

in subsequent patristic literature.[6] That the Mother of God should have to be under the dominion of sin until she was redeemed and sanctified at the foot of the cross not only offends what Christians, East and West, have thought of her, but it contradicts the spirit and the letter of the Gospel's account of the annunciation, in which Mary is greeted by Gabriel as "full of grace [κεχαριτωμένη]" and "blessed among women," as "having found favor [χάριν] with God," so that "the Lord is with" her (Luke 1:28–30). How could she, upon whom the Holy Spirit came and who was overshadowed by the power of the Most High, be under sin? We feel like asking Paul's question: "What accord has Christ with Belial?" (2 Cor 6:15).

Hence, the received opinion in Orthodox minds is that the Virgin Mary's sanctification occurred at the precise moment of the annunciation.[7] This middle-ground solution stands in the equipoise between the two alternative positions—the position of a later time, favored by Origen, and the position of an earlier time, affirmed by the doctrine of the immaculate conception. As such, it creates a unique ambiguity. Is Mary exempt from the state of sin under which the rest of humanity finds itself, and thus not in need of Christ's redemptive work that flows from his cross? If not, how are we to understand a sanctification that precedes that by which we are sanctified? And how do we understand that sanctification in question?

It should be clear that there is a difference between the holiness of the various saints of both the Old and New Testaments and that of the Virgin Mary. She is most holy (παναγία) and the first among the saints that the Church commemorates.[8] It is one of the ironies of history that, at the high point of the theological conflict between East and West, it was the Patriarch of Constantinople Michael I (Cerularios) who protested the "Latin" custom of referring to and invoking the Virgin Mary simply as *Sancta Maria*—an appellation that, in the eyes of the Eastern churches, failed to underscore

---

6. With the notable exception of Cyril of Alexandria (see PG 74:661B), who adopts the idea of Mary's scandal at the crucifixion.

7. On this opinion, see Spourlakou-Eutychiadou, "Most Holy Theotokos," 336–40. M. Jugie in his authoritative study on the subject, *L'Immaculée Conception dans l'Ecriture Sainte*, demonstrates that this view is predominately a sixteenth-century construction.

8. Liturgically the priority of Mary in the communion of saints is expressed most emphatically in the anaphora of the Byzantine liturgies (St. Basil's and St. John Chrysostom's), in which she is commemorated not only first but "above all else" (ἐξαιρέτως τῆς παναγίας, ἀχράντου καὶ ὑπερευλογημένης, ἐνδόξου, δεσποίνης ἡμῶν, Θεοτόκου καὶ ἀειπαρθένου Μαρίας . . .). There can be no more solemn confirmation of Mary's titles than this.

the exceptional holiness of Mary.[9] The exception that the Church perceived in the holiness of the Virgin Mary was eloquently summarized by St. Sophronius, Patriarch of Jerusalem, in one of his homilies on the Annunciation of the Virgin. "Many became saints before you," St. Sophronius has Gabriel saying to the Virgin:

> But no one was full of grace like you; no one was blessed like you; no one was sanctified like you; no one was magnified like you; no one was purified in advance like you; no one was enlightened like you; no one was illuminated like you; no one was exalted like you; no one brought God forward like you; no one became so rich in God's gifts like you; no one received God's grace like you; you exceed in every human excellence . . .[10]

So much for Mary's state of exception which, paradoxically, reveals to us the rule of the divine law for all humanity. This question, then, arises: Was the Virgin Mary so sanctified because she conceived the Lord, or is it rather that she conceived the Lord because she was sanctified? This dilemma can be entertained only under the prism of temporal sequence; from a timeless viewpoint, however, both possibilities converge to a hendiadys of grace. To put it differently, the relation of Mary's holiness to him who "alone is holy" is a relation of both efficient and final cause: she is sanctified because she gives birth to God *and* in order to do so. Patristic evidence speaks quite unambiguously in favor of the latter: as the incarnation of the Logos was not an afterthought in God's plan so the birth of the woman who was to be the central person in the realization of that mystery was carefully planned—indeed, as we will see, before all ages.

Already since the time of Irenaeus of Lyon, Mary was seen in the broad context of the fall and future restoration of mankind, and therefore an understanding of her role began invariably with a typological reading of Genesis. As Adam, the first man, came from the virgin earth of Eden, so Christ, the new Adam, took flesh in the virgin womb of Mary. Mary is also the new Eve, mother of a humanity restored to its prelapsarian glory:

---

9. See Louth, *Greek East and Latin West*, 310.

10. Sophronius, *Oratio II (Ad Annuntiationem)*, PG 87/3, 3248A. The Greek reads as follows: Πολλοὶ μὲν πρὸ σοῦ γεγόνασιν ἅγιοι, ἀλλ' οὐδεὶς κατὰ σὲ κεχαρίτωται, οὐδεὶς κατὰ σὲ μεμακάρισται, οὐδεὶς κατὰ σὲ καθηγίασται, οὐδεὶς κατὰ σὲ μεμεγάλυνται, οὐδεὶς κατὰ σὲ προκεκάθαρται, οὐδεὶς κατὰ σὲ περιηύγασται, οὐδεὶς κατὰ σὲ ἐκπεφώτισται, οὐδεὶς κατὰ σὲ ὑπερύψωται, οὐδεὶς κατὰ σὲ Θεῷ προσεπέλασε, καὶ οὐδεὶς κατὰ σὲ Θεοῦ δώροις πεπλούτηκεν, οὐδεὶς κατὰ σὲ Θεοῦ χάριν ἐδέξατο, πάντα νικᾷς τὰ παρὰ ἀνθρώποις ἐξαίρετα . . .

> For just as [Eve] was led astray by the word of an angel, so that she fled from God when she had transgressed His word; so did [Mary], by an angelic communication, receive the glad tidings that she should sustain God, being obedient to His word. And if the former did disobey God, yet the latter was persuaded to be obedient to God, in order that the Virgin Mary might become the patroness of the virgin Eve. And thus, as the human race fell into bondage to death by means of a virgin, so is it rescued by a virgin; virginal disobedience having been balanced in the opposite scale by virginal obedience.[11]

Because Eve is a typological adumbration of Mary, the Fathers of the Church understood Mary as announced already in the beginning of the Old Testament, as chosen, prepared, and preserved by God to become the sanctified vessel of his epiphany in history. Appropriately, then, we first meet this concept in the famous sermon that St. Gregory the Theologian (Nazianzen) delivered on the feast of the Epiphany. At a time in the Church's history when Marian doctrine was still very much nascent, St. Gregory speaks quite boldly of the Virgin Mary as "having both soul and flesh pre-purified [προκαθαρθείσης] by the Spirit."[12] What calls for a hermeneutical examination is the prefix *pre*-: the Virgin was not simply "purified," but "pre-purified." Does St. Gregory have in mind the time of the annunciation or a still earlier time? The answer to this question is given by two Fathers of uncontested authority in the Orthodox Church: John of Damascus and Photius, Patriarch of Constantinople.

In a sermon rich with theological insights delivered on the feast of the Virgin's Nativity, John of Damascus explains how Mary was preordained to minister to the mystery of humanity's salvation through God's incarnation: "For you did not live in yourself, inasmuch as you did not come to being for your own sake. You lived in God; for whom you came to life, so that you may tend the universal salvation, so that God's ancient decision of the Word's humanization and of our divinization may become fulfilled through you."[13] Thus Mary is the "tree of life" which, although planted in Paradise,

---

11. Irenaeus, *Against Heresies* (V, 19, 1), in *Ante-Nicene Fathers*, 1:547.

12. Gregory Nazianzen, *Oration 38* (*On Theophany*), PG 36:325. The same passage is repeated verbatim in his Easter homily (*Oration 45*), PG 36:633. For an original and in-depth analysis of the theology of προκαθαρθεῖσα (which, interestingly enough, was translated into Latin already since that time as *immaculata*) and of all the relevant patristic texts, from Nazianzen to Mark Eugenicus, see Kappes, *The Immaculate Conception*.

13. John of Damascus, *Sermo in Nativitatem Sanctae Dei Genitricis Mariae*, in *Die Schriften des Johannes von Damaskos*, 179.

does not bear fruit—the fruit of her womb (cf. Luke 1:42)—except "at a time preordained by God."[14] In the vista that Mary's cosmic mystery opens for the homilist, the Damascene sees the ages of human history competing with each other, each desiring to claim for itself the pride of being the one to witness her nativity; yet it was God's "preordained decision" (ἡ προωρισμένη βουλὴ τοῦ Θεοῦ) that prevailed in the end, and so the last times came first (alluding to Matt 19:30), for it was during the last times (οἱ ἔσχατοι) that the Virgin was born.[15] Thus, in a masterful oratorical rendition of Rom 8:30, the Damascene concludes, "The God of all, having foreknown you to be worthy, he also loved you, and having loved you, he also predestined you, and at the end of times he brought you to being, and he revealed you to be a God-bearing mother and maid of his own Son and Word."[16] Lastly, the significance of Mary's ministry in the mystery of humanity's salvation necessitated for John of Damascus that "she was preserved immaculate, a spouse for God and a mother for God's natural Son."[17] The Damascene's laudation expresses clearly that God did not choose Mary because she was holy—for grace would not have been grace anymore—but rather she is made holy because she was chosen to become the Mother of God. It is also expressly stated that Mary's sanctification did not take place later in her life, neither at the foot of the cross nor by the greeting of the angel, but she was sanctified by God when God preordained the mystery of the humanization of the Logos: before all ages. In doing so, the Eastern homiletic tradition reconfirms in this case as well a theological principle common to both Catholic and Orthodox Christianity that has been seldom noticed and little discussed, even though it underlines every major dogmatic area of theology, namely, the principle of theological maximalism which has been

---

14. Ibid.

15. The predestination of Mary has been codified in the liturgy for the feast of her nativity. In the *kontakion* for the forefeast we read: Ἡ παρθένος σήμερον, καὶ θεοτόκος Μαρία, ἡ παστὰς ἡ ἄλυτος, τοῦ οὐρανίου Νυμφίου, τίκεται ἀπὸ τῆς στείρας θεοβουλήτως, ὄχημα τοῦ θεοῦ Λόγου εὐτρεπισθῆναι, εἰς τοῦτο γὰρ καὶ προωρίσθη, ἡ θεία πύλη, καὶ Μήτηρ τῆς ὄντως ζωῆς. It is worth noticing here that the Virgin Mary is predestined (προωρίσθη) by God's will (θεοβουλήτως) to become the vehicle of God the Logos.

16. John of Damascus, *Sermo in Nativitatem*: Σὲ προγνοὺς ὁ τῶν ὅλων θεὸς ἀξίαν ἠγάπησε καὶ ἀγαπήσας προώρισε καὶ ἐπ' ἐσχάτων τῶν χρόνων εἰς τὸ εἶναι παρήγαγε καὶ θεοτόκον μητέρα καὶ τιθηνὸν τοῦ οἰκείου υἱοῦ καὶ λόγου ἀνέδειξε. Ibid., 177.

17. John of Damascus, *Sermo in Nativitatem*: . . . τηρηθὲν ἄμωμον εἰς νύμφην θεοῦ καὶ μητέρα τοῦ φύσει υἱοῦ τοῦ θεοῦ. Ibid., 176.

summarized by Jaroslav Pelikan with the expression "better to believe and teach too much than too little."[18]

The second text we have chosen, taken also from a sermon from the feast of the Virgin's Nativity (September 8th), is even more unambiguous. "It was necessary," writes St. Photius with an expression reminiscent of Duns Scotus's decisive *decuit*,[19] "it was necessary that such a Mother be preordained for the Creator—a Mother that preserved from the very swaddling clothes her body pure, her soul pure, pure also the thoughts and not only the words."[20] This is why, when the angel comes to announce to her the good news of the Savior's conception, he finds her already pure: "The Holy Spirit will come down upon you, *the immaculate*, making you even more pure."[21]

Thus, Mary is revealed as the example, if you wish, of the new humanity in Christ—an eschatological person, or rather, the kind of person we are all destined to be eschatologically. The eschaton came to history by and through the incarnation of our Lord, who repeats about himself that he is the kingdom of God which has come to us and among us,[22] in the *pleroma* of time, that is, in the fullness of time.[23] We cannot say this and then try to explain the immaculate conception of the Virgin Mary *biologically*, that is, by the categories of the fallen world, as if Christ had not come to the world. What I mean by this is simply that Mary's birth, understood as free from

18. Pelikan, *Mary Through the Centuries*, 196.

19. Duns Scotus's maximalist solution to the debate on the immaculate conception was codified in the formula *potuit, decuit, fecit*, that is, "whatever was both possible and eminently fitting for God to do, that he did." In Pelikan, *Mary Through the Centuries*, 196.

20. Photius of Constantinople, *Oratio in Sanctissime dei Genitricis natalem diem*: Ἔδει γὰρ, ἔδει τὴν ἐξ αὐτῶν σπαργάνων ἁγνὸν μὲν τὸ σῶμα, ἁγνὴν δὲ τὴν ψυχήν, ἁγνοὺς δὲ τοὺς λογισμούς, κρεῖττον ἢ λόγῳ, συντηρήσασαν, Μητέρα ταύτην προορισθῆναι τοῦ Πλάσαντος (PG 102:560).

21. Sophronius of Jerusalem, *Oratio II. In Deiparae Annuntiationem*: Πνεῦμα ἅγιον ἐπὶ σὲ, τὴν ἀμόλυντον, κάτεισι, καθαρωτέραν σε ποιησόμενον (PG 87:3273). The last expression, καθαρωτέραν, does not intend to denote comparative gradation of purity, especially as no object of comparison follows; it is rather a common rhetorical trope for expressing superabundance. Again, the language of Eastern liturgy is replete with examples of expressing superabundance or excellence by the comparative. The first that comes to mind and that uses the very term in question here is a τροπάριον of the ninth ode from the intercessory canon to the Theotokos: τὴν ὑψηλοτέραν τῶν οὐρανῶν, καὶ καθαρωτέραν, λαμπηδόνων ἡλιακῶν ... ("Higher than the heavens above are you, and you are much purer than the radiance of the sun ...").

22. So Luke 17:21, "because the kingdom of God is in your midst."

23. Mark 1:15; Gal 4:4.

the original sin (being, subsequently, free from any sin), is the result of Christ's work as redeemer, as the One who brings the eschaton in history in order to change history. Yet, one might object, Mary's birth takes place *before* Christ's: how can *her* birth be the result of his? Truly, Mary gives birth to Christ, but in another, more profound sense, *it is Christ who "gives birth" to Mary and, through her, to all humanity.* The concept of prevenient grace (προδραμούσα χάρις) implies that God's grace is not restricted by time, or, at least, by our conception of forward-moving time. Eschatologically speaking, an event of the past can be caused by what happens in the present, or even by what has not yet taken place. It is this paradox that the Fourth Gospel expresses in the formula "the hour is coming and is now here" (John 4:23; 5:25). Christian eschatology has indeed such a retroactive effect. Is not, for example, the Transfiguration of the Lord on Mt. Tabor the proleptic enactment in the "already" of that which, for us, is "not yet"? Is it not the Lord's resurrection the result as much as the adumbration of the common resurrection at the end of times?[24] In the Virgin Mary's birth, as in her death, we see the light of the end of times breaking into history and transforming its categories.[25] No church, Catholic or Orthodox, can afford sacrificing so much by denying such an essential summation of Christian doctrine. Thankfully, neither does. Whatever protestations *some* Orthodox theologians have raised in criticism of the immaculate conception of the Theotokos has been insignificant with respect to the points we have articulated here, for they simply ignore or fail to properly understand what is essential in it, misunderstanding it, instead, as some arbitrary distortion and novelty, invented in order to explain the Lord's immaculate birth, while in reality, as we have shown, it is explained by it.

Finally, when we affirm that the Virgin Mary was, indeed, in need of God's prevenient grace for her sanctification at the moment of her conception we have affirmed in the most emphatic way the *difference* between her and the redeemer himself, whose virginal conception was in no need whatsoever of such a remedy. Freedom from sin was for him by nature, while for her by grace, by the very grace of him whom she bore in a manner exceptional in nature. "For it is one thing to be God and quite another to participate in God. God is by nature unable to sin, but one who participates

---

24. "If there is no resurrection of the dead, then not even Christ has been raised" (1 Cor 15:13). See also my article "The Anarchic Principle of Christian Eschatology."

25. On the retroactive effect of the eschatological, especially with reference to Christ's transfiguration, see the conclusion of chapter four below (64–68).

in God receives it from God that he is unable to sin."²⁶ In this respect, too, we see Mary as the exemplar and promise of our eschatological condition, for it is such felicitous inability that our freewill will enjoy at the end of times as a gift and effect of its participation in God.

---

26. Augustine, *City of God*, XXII.30 (Babcock, 552).

Two

The Procession of the Holy Spirit

OUR NEXT ISSUE FINDS the positions of both churches, in the opinion of this author, somewhat problematic. I speak, of course, of the procession of the Holy Spirit. There is no need to refer here to the historical reasons that led to the addition of the now famously controversial *filioque* to the Creed. The addition of this phrase sought to solve a problem before it inadvertently created another. I am not concerned with the addition itself, even though in my eyes it was a harmful decision in the history of the Church. It is a well-known fact that Pope Leo III, as late as 810, refused the addition of the *filioque*, officially proposed by Charlemagne, and rather had the text of the Creed without the *filioque* engraved in Latin and Greek on two silver plaques that were hung on each side of St. Peter's altar.[1] Today the *filioque* clause is not obligatory for the Eastern-rite Catholics, and it has been omitted from the text of the Creed by a decision of the Greek Catholic hierarchy (May 31, 1973). Both Popes John Paul II and Benedict XVI omitted the *filioque* on occasion—when reciting the Nicene Creed together with the Ecumenical Patriarch, or in the presence of "other representatives of the Ecumenical Throne"[2]—and at least one illustrious Catholic theologian was in favor of a universal suspension of the clause.[3] The theological commis-

---

1. See Congar, *I Believe in the Holy Spirit*, 3:53. Congar follows similar recommendations made by Garrigues and Bouyer.
2. Nichols, *Rome and the Eastern Churches*, 260.
3. Congar, *I Believe in the Holy Spirit*, 3:206. I cannot agree with Fr. Nichols's efforts that seek to exonerate the addition of the controversial clause in the creed (see *Rome and the Eastern Churches*, 251–60).

Part One—Revisiting Theological Differences

sion Faith and Order of the World Council of Churches held two meetings in Klingenthal, in which Catholic theologians also participated, that discussed the old controversy and came to the resolution of restoring the Nicene Creed without the addition of the *filioque*.[4]

I would like, however, to say something about the doctrine itself that declares that the third person of the Holy Trinity proceeds from the Father *and the Son*. This doctrine was a well-intended attempt, no doubt, to solve one of the deepest mysteries of our faith that might as well be left unresolved. The mystery in question concerns the relationship between the Son and the Holy Spirit. Revelation and the Church's tradition have sufficiently identified the relation of the Father with the Son, on the one hand, and of the Father with the Holy Spirit, on the other. To the former we refer by the name of "begetting," to the latter by the name of "proceeding" (ἐκπόρευσις), or more specifically of "spiration." These names tell us nothing more than that the Holy Trinity is a communion of persons, a communion that affirms oneness while at the same time upholding otherness, and that the source of these communal relations is the person of the Father whom the Creed identifies as the One God ("the monarchy of the Father"[5]). Catholic theology, always more concerned with clarity and completeness than its Orthodox counterpart, sensed early on that a third relation, namely that between the Son and the Holy Spirit, was left unidentified. Historically, its answer to this doctrinal lacuna was simply to duplicate the relation between the Father and the Holy Spirit and assign that very same relation, namely procession, between the Son and the Holy Spirit as well ("and from the Son"). This was the best that it could do, on the basis of scriptural testimony, and taking as a model for the inner life of the Holy Trinity ("immanent Trinity") the way the Holy Trinity was revealed to us in the plan of our salvation ("economic

---

4. The meetings were held in 1978 and 1979. The proceedings were published in the volume *Spirit of God, Spirit of Christ*. An appraisal of the contributions made by the commission, from an Orthodox point of view, can be found in Theodore Stylianopoulos' "The *Filioque*: Dogma, Theologoumenon or Error?" In his account of the symposium, Fr. Aidan Nichols is rather critical of its conclusions (*Rome and the Eastern Churches*, 251–52).

5. See Gregory Nazianzen, *Third Theological Oration*, 130, and *Fifth Theological Oration*, 244, in *Die fünf theologischen Reden*. The identification of God's oneness with the person of the Father was, according to Metropolitan John of Pergamon (Zizioulas), one of the two fundamental "leavenings," as he calls them, of patristic theology. For the history of this ground-breaking association and its theological implications, see his *Being as Communion*, 40. See also chapter 3, "The Father as Cause," in his *Communion and Otherness*, 113–54.

The Procession of the Holy Spirit

Trinity").[6] On the other hand, Orthodox theology only recently became aware of the problem that Catholic theologians had tried to address already since the Middle Ages. Furthermore, it is an unfortunate circumstance of history that Orthodox theologians, even before they became aware of the problem as such, reacted polemically against its proposed solution. A notable exception is St. Maximus the Confessor, who, in his letter to Marinus, offers an irenic explanation of the matter.[7] Thus, the current state of scholarship leaves the Orthodox with no position on this subject: for either they deny the Catholic position of the procession of the Holy Spirit from the Son, but without so much as suggesting an alternative, or, in reaction to the Catholic solution, they affirm that the Holy Spirit proceeds *only* from the Father,[8] leaving again the problem of identifying the relationship between the Son and the Holy Spirit fundamentally untouched.

One should note, however, that the question of the procession of the Holy Spirit becomes a controversy between East and West much later than either the formulation of the doctrine that dates back to St. Augustine or the addition of the clause in the Creed. It was not regarded as controversial by the Eastern Church and its Fathers—again, the case of St. Maximus is a good example—until the two churches had already begun falling apart on other matters. In other words, such a mystery as the procession of the Holy

---

6. I disagree with Karl Rahner's famous *Grundaxiom* that identifies the economic Trinity with the immanent Trinity—God as revealed *to us* and *in history* cannot, by definition, be one and the same as God is *in se*. For Rahner's axiom, see *Theological Investigations*, 4:77–102.

7. "Just as the Holy Spirit exists by his nature according to the essence of God the Father, so too does he exist by his nature according to the essence of the Son insofar as he proceeds essentially from the Father through the begotten Son. They [the Latins of Rome] have shown that they have not made the Son the cause of the Spirit. They know, in fact, that the Father is the only cause of the Son and the Spirit, of the first by begetting and of the second by *ekporeusis* [original procession]. They have, however, pointed to the procession through him and have shown in this way the unity and identity of the divine essence." PG 91:136, translation in Congar, *I Believe in the Holy Spirit*, 3:200–201.

8 See, for example, Photius's addition in his *Mystagogia* of the formula "ἐκ μόνου τοῦ πατρός" regarding the procession of the Holy Spirit (PG 102:263–400)—an addition that was certainly as arbitrary and polemical an innovation as the *filioque* some centuries earlier. By this addition, Photius sought to create a new dogmatic position for Eastern pneumatology, namely, that the Holy Spirit proceeds *only* from the Father, or from the Father *alone*, the not-so-silent implication being that the Second Person of the Holy Trinity is not involved in any way (either *from* him or *through* him) in the procession of the Holy Spirit. For an Orthodox criticism of Photius's *monopatrism*, see Bulgakov, *The Comforter*, in particular 97–100 and 137–38, and Balthasar, *Theo-Logic III: The Spirit of Truth*, 214–15.

Spirit was dragged into the mud of the polemics between the two sides in order not to cause but to justify an estrangement already underway. It came to serve as an accusation that either side could throw at the other, precisely when such an accusation was needed. It became an excellent example of theology at the service of political divisions. It should not be surprising, therefore, that no other theological literature produced over the course of church history is less inspiring than, ironically, that which was written on the procession of the Holy Spirit. Reading the polemical works on either side of the debate, one cannot find anything positive, not even that unintentional good which has been said to arise from heresies—namely that, in demanding a response, they stir the Church to better define its doctrine and sharpen its theological acumen. No such positive outcome can be credited to the *filioque* controversy. Rather, some of the better minds of their times heaped up words, treatise after treatise, in the service of a futile and hateful debate. We ought to know better today and so not follow them in this path of self-destruction.

On the other hand, I would not even dream of suggesting an answer to this problem, before which better minds than mine remained reverently silent. I suspect that the theological difficulty has something to do with the person of the Holy Spirit himself, who, even though he glorifies the Son and together with the Son reveals the Father, never seeks his own, never calls attention to himself, but remains, as every holy person in whom he dwells, self-effaced and evasive. It also has something to do with the circumstances under which it was investigated: for a matter pertaining to the sustainer of the Church's unity was approached in the spirit of animosity among brothers. Whenever love has grown cold, one cannot find consent of minds either: it is not accidental that before the profession of faith the liturgy asks of us to "love one another that with one mind we may confess Father, Son, and Holy Spirit, Trinity consubstantial and indivisible."

Nevertheless—and in keeping with a theological axiom that will become explicit in the next section and that recapitulates in a nutshell the character of Eastern theology, namely, the principle of the centrality of the person in theology, Christology, and ecclesiology—I would like to offer my support to an irenic solution suggested by the Dominican theologian Jean-Miguel Garrigues in his work *L'Esprit qui dit "Père!": L'Esprit-Saint dans la vie trinitaire et le problème du Filioque*. Garrigues upholds the person of the Father as the source of both (consubstantial) communion and (hypostatic) otherness in the Holy Trinity. As Aidan Nichols notes, the implications of this simple yet indispensable principle for the controversy of the *filioque* can be far-reaching, as it differentiates between

> three senses in which the Father is the source of the Godhead. He is (a) source of the divine nature, (b) source of the consubstantial communion of the persons, and (c) source of the hypostatic diversity of the Son and the Spirit. In sense (b) the Western form of the Creed is the better form; in sense (c) the Greek form is preferable. But these senses are not contradictory; rather, they are complementary.⁹

If we now add to the above the linguistic differentiation between the Latin term *procedere* and the Greek term ἐκπορεύεσθαι—two terms that cannot be taken as synonymous, as the former implies a connection and continuity (closer to the concept of περιχώρησις in Greek theological parlance), while the latter denotes a distinction (better captured as a procession strongly qualified, in the sense that St. Augustine does in *De Trinitate* XV.4.29),¹⁰ then, I think, the two views, Greek and Latin, on the procession of the Holy Spirit could become harmonized.

St. Augustine's passage mentioned above reads as follows:

> Only the Father is called the one from whom the Word is born and from whom the Holy Spirit principally [*principaliter*] proceeds. I added "principally," because we have found that the Holy Spirit also proceeds from the Son. But this too was given the Son by the Father—not given to him when he already existed and did not yet have it; but whatever the Father gave to his only-begotten Word he gave by begetting him. He so begot him then that their common gift [*donum commune*] would proceed from him too, and the Holy Spirit would be the Spirit of them both.¹¹

It is clear that St. Augustine distinguishes in this passage between two distinct kinds of processions—for which, unfortunately, the same term is employed, facilitating thus the ensuing confusion.¹² On the one hand, we

---

9. Nichols, *Rome and the Eastern Churches*, 265.

10. Ibid., 267. "Garrigues has been at great pains to exhibit a credible etymological distinction between *ekporeuomai* and *pro-cedere* (which actually means 'to retreat forward,' the Greek *pro-chorein*)." Balthasar, *Theo-Logic III: The Spirit of Truth*, 211.

11. Augustine, *The Trinity*, XV.4.29 (Hill, 419).

12. Why is it that the same (Latin) term is employed in naming two distinct relations? "Simply because the Latin Bible used [*procedere*] in place of several Greek verbs in the Gospels at relevant points. Already at Florence, the Easterners had noted how few terms the Latin had for the relations of origin." Nichols, *Rome and the Eastern Churches*, 266.

Part One—Revisiting Theological Differences

have the procession of the Holy Spirit from the Father *principaliter*. This qualification reserves this kind of procession exclusively for the Father precisely as the only *principium* or ἀρχή of the Holy Trinity (Maximus Planudes translates *principaliter* as ἀρχοειδῶς);[13] thus, the Greek insistence on the μοναρχία of the Father is preserved and upheld.[14] As distinguished from the former, the Holy Spirit's "procession" from the Son cannot anymore be understood as a procession strictly speaking, that is, as ἐκπόρευσις, but rather as a πρόοδος. The doctrine of the Holy Spirit's double "going forth" (πρόοδος)—one hypostatic from the Father, the other communicative from the Father *and the Son*—is based, according to one Orthodox scholar of late Byzantine theology, on "the ancient Eastern, Cappadocian, and Palamite distinction between divine essence and divine energies."[15] It is hard to see how the Palamite distinction between essence and energies relates to the question of the procession of the Holy Spirit without committing the mistake of reading the economic Trinity back into the intratrinitarian relationships. The same can be said about the proposed (Eastern) concession that the Son ἐκφαίνει (reveals, makes manifest) the Holy Spirit. For such a revelation would presuppose a recipient of what is hereby revealed. Thus we are already transported to history and *economia*.

How is it that we should understand that second "procession" is indicated by St. Augustine's own qualification of a *donum commune*: it is, in other words, within the context of Trinitarian communion that the Holy Spirit can be said to be "of the Son" and "from the Son." And Garrigues is right in suggesting, as we have seen, that the Orthodox should be expected to understand and accept this reading if presented to them under the proper term of *perichoresis*.

---

13. Augustine, Περὶ Τριάδος, II, 933. By the year 1283 the Byzantine scholar Maximos Planudes had completed the Greek translation of St. Augustine's work *On the Trinity*. It is through this translation that later on St. Gregory Palamas will come to know the work of St. Augustine.

14. An insistence that characterizes almost every single polemical work written on the subject of the Holy Spirit's procession by an Orthodox theologian. For some examples of late Byzantine authorship, see the collection of polemical works assembled by Andronikos Demetrakopoulos (by such authors as Ioannes Fournes, Eustratios of Nicaea, Nikolaos of Methone, Nikephoros Blemmydes, and Georgios Akropolites) in *Bibliotheca Ecclesiastica*.

15. Ioannides, Ο Ιωσὴφ Βρυέννιος: Βίος-Ἔργα-Διδασκαλία, 207.

Three

The Petrine Primacy

THE QUESTION OF PETRINE primacy is, among the issues discussed here, the one with the most relevancy, first of all because it is currently under examination by the Joint International Commission on the Theological Dialogue between the two churches, and second, because both foregoing issues—the doctrine of the immaculate conception and the *filioque*—are problematic in the eyes of the Orthodox ultimately not in themselves, but to the extent that they exemplify the pope's primacy and authority to define and promulgate Christian dogma.[1] Thus, in discussing the primacy of the pope, we have reached the core of what was really at stake in our discussion so far. For these reasons, we will dedicate to it a lengthier treatment. It is also the question that posits itself with the most urgency for the Orthodox churches, which, in the absence of a unity concretely manifested

---

1. Marcus Plested, for example, in his recent valuable treatment of the Orthodox reception of Thomas Aquinas, notices how the debate over the *filioque* was linked historically with that of the papal primacy; thus, he writes of "the *filioque* and the organically related question of papal primacy" or of "the *filioque* and the related question of papal primacy" (*Orthodox Readings of Aquinas*, 22 and 25). Similarly, the doctrine of the immaculate conception was connected with the polemics against the primacy of the pope already since 1848 (as in the *Encyclical of the Four Patriarchs*); see ibid., 186. Both issues were considered examples of a primacy that was understood only in terms of powers, especially the power to define dogma unilaterally and—so it was perceived—arbitrarily. Aidan Nichols voices the opinion that "at root, only one issue of substance divides the Orthodox and the Catholic Churches, and that is the issue of the primacy" (*Rome and the Eastern Churches*, 313).

by a *primus*, face the dire consequences of inter-Orthodox disagreements, conflicts, and even schisms.[2]

The need for primacy cannot be denied; it is demanded not only by the structure of the Church but also from the experience of ecclesial and ecclesiastical life. Since communion with Rome and its primate was lost for the Orthodox churches, we have struggled to maintain our unity either in terms of a common faith (and this, in the wake of the schism, has meant almost invariably an identity solidified by anti-Latin sentiments) or in terms of our common liturgical customs and rites, or, more recently, by appealing to the democratic idea of a "federation" of churches, allegedly all equal among themselves, expressed by pan-Orthodox councils. Thus, Papadakis writes, "Christendom indeed was both a diversity and a unity, a family of basically equally sister-Churches, whose unity rested not on any visible juridical authority, but on conciliarity, and on common declaration of faith and sacramental life."[3] Some preliminary remarks on the misunderstanding that finds expression in this passage: first, there cannot be a council without a *primus* who convokes and presides over it, and therefore, conciliarity presupposes primacy; second, the very metaphor of "sister-Churches" implies a mother church, that is, again, a see invested with primacy; as for the common declaration of faith and sacramental life, this is perhaps the feeblest of all arguments brought forward against primacy for reasons that become evident later on, and it is not corroborated by the *development* of liturgy in the East, as discussed by the same author.[4]

I would like to argue that such attempts to Orthodox unity are not only ineffective (as the sin of ethnophyletism bitterly reminds us) but also against the Church's theology.[5] They are against the Church's theology be-

---

2. Examples abound: perhaps the most scandalous case is that of the diaspora where multiple Orthodox jurisdictions overlap, distinguished only by their ethnicity. Thus, in western Europe, the Americas, and Australia one finds in the same locality Russian Orthodox, Antiochean Orthodox, Serbian Orthodox, and Romanian Orthodox churches. This problematic situation gives rise to all kind of conflicts: from bishops who claim the same title (e.g., "of Buenos Aires," or "of Boston") to schisms (a recent example being the decision of the Patriarchate of Antioch to sever communion with the Patriarchate of Jerusalem over a parish in Qatar that both patriarchates claim as belonging to their jurisdictions).

3. Papadakis, *Christian East*, 159–60.

4. Ibid., 310–14.

5. I am following here the argument that I discussed in my essay "Primacy and Ecclesiology." For an account that traces the historical developments that led to the fragmentation of the Eastern Church's "commonwealth" into its present-day pitiful state, see Nichols, *Rome and the Eastern Churches*, 143–50.

cause they seek to effect unity by means other than that of the *person*, while for our theology, Eastern and Western, unity—whether we speak of the oneness of the Holy Trinity, or of the hypostatic oneness of Christ's two natures, or of the oneness of the faithful assembled in the celebration of the Eucharist—is always effected by means of a person. It is the person of the Father who vouchsafes the oneness of the Holy Trinity; it is the person of the incarnate Logos that safeguards the unity of his two natures "without confusion and without division," as the Fourth Ecumenical Council proclaimed; it is the person of the bishop who maintains the unity of the ecclesial body, so that they may confess their belief in "One, Holy, Catholic, and Apostolic church."

In all things in the Church there is *taxis*—that is, sequential order—as St. Gregory the Theologian reminds us;[6] and order implies an ordering of things, that is, a hierarchy. It is such hierarchical ordering that gives to each thing and to each one a proper place. When everything has its proper place in the cosmos around us as well as in the microcosm inside us, then beauty and truth are allowed to shine forth, to show themselves in the unfolding of that order. In the Church this unfolding takes the form of what the great Renaissance philosopher and cardinal Nicholas of Cusa has called an *explicatio Petri*[7]—the unfolding of Peter—an unfolding that takes place not only through the ages, horizontally so to speak, but also vertically, through the three levels around which the Church is structured: the local, the eparchial, and the universal. As for the first two, the local and the eparchial, there is a primacy embodied in the person of the bishop and the archbishop or

---

6. "Τάξιν θεολογίας" (*Fifth Theological Oration*, in *Die fünf theologischen Reden*, 264). Such a *taxis* is reflected in all of the catalogues of the twelve apostles given to us by the gospels (Matt 10; Mark 3; Luke 6). So Matthew writes, "These are the names of the twelve apostles: *first* [πρῶτος] Simon who is called Peter, and Andrew, his brother, and James son of Zebedee, and his brother John" (Matt 10:2). In spite of the slight variations in the ordering of the names among the different Synoptic Gospels (to which one could add the narrative of John 1:40–49 as well as the list of the twelve given in Acts 1:13–14, to which now Mary, the Mother of God, is also included), what is important in these lists is two fundamental points: *a*) that there is such an order (*taxis*), a sort of apostolic hierarchy, and *b*) that in all the catalogues the first name is that of Peter. Matthew's account is particularly telling as he explicitly names Peter as first (πρῶτος). Undoubtedly, then, there is a πρῶτος, a *primus*, among the apostles. See also Nicholas of Cusa, *Writings on Church and Reform*, 117.

7. Nicholas of Cusa, "Letter to Rodrigo Sanchez de Arevalo," in *Writings on Church and Reform*, 437.

metropolitan respectively, and so in the third level, that of the universal, there is a primacy embodied in the person of the bishop of Rome.[8]

> For it is fitting for the sensible Church to have a sensible head; and, for this reason, the sensible head of this Church is the pontiff, who is chosen from among men. In him this Church exists in an enfolded manner as in the first confessor of Christ. We know that Peter was the first confessor of Christ among men; and for this reason Peter, who received his name from confessing the Rock who is Christ, unfolded the Church enfolded in himself first of all through the word of doctrine.[9]

It is important at this point to resist the temptation of differentiating between Peter's faith and Peter himself, as some Orthodox theologians have attempted to do, in order to avoid understanding the words of Christ in Matt 16:18 ("Thou are Peter, and upon this rock I will build my church") as referring to Peter's person and, by implication, to his successors. Thus, Gregory Zigavinos—and those who follow him in this polemical interpretation—understands the "rock" upon which Christ builds his church to be Peter's confession.[10] Yet, is it possible to separate the confession from the confessor? Is there a faith that is not hypostasized in a concrete and particular person? The centrality of the person's role for the question of primacy should become evident later on. For now, let us return to Cusanus's analysis.

> Since, however, a multitude can participate [in] unity only in a varied diversity, the Church cannot subsist, consequently, except in a varied participation of unity. For this reason it is necessary for there to be various members of the only body of the Church, in whom there is that one whole confession in the whole and in

---

8. "Thus, after the first part—the main theme of which is the spiritual basis of the principle of unity—Möhler is able to develop in the second part the increasingly concrete steps by which manifest unity is built from below: unity (for the community) in the bishop, unity of the bishops in the metropolitan and in (local) synods and unity of the entire episcopate (Cyprian) summed up in the 'unity in the primate' as the symbol of episcopal unity in its 'living representative.'" Balthasar, *Office of Peter*, 169. Balthasar's reference in this passage is to Johann Adam Möhler's work *Die Einheit in der Kirche* (1825). This position was most recently adopted by the Ravenna Statement ("Ecclesiological and Canonical Consequences of the Sacramental Nature of the Church: Ecclesial Communion, Conciliarity and Authority") issued by the Joint International Commission for the Theological Dialogue between the Roman Catholic Church and the Orthodox Church. For a discussion of the Ravenna Statement, see McPartlan, *A Service of Love*.

9. Nicholas of Cusa, *Writings on Church and Reform*, 437.

10. Vgenopoulos (now Metropolitan of Selyvria), *Primacy in the Church*, 44.

every part of it. The Church, therefore, exists as a unity in a varied diversity. And just as the virtue of unity cannot be attained except in a participated diversity, so the virtue of the enfolding principle can be grasped only in things unfolded from the principle. . . . In this way, moreover, the enfolded virtue of Peter as the head of the Church cannot be grasped except in the Church unfolded from him.[11]

Cusanus's highly metaphysical and mystical ecclesiology of the Petrine unfolding might sound strange to our ears, accustomed as we are to approaching ecclesiological questions only from a "pragmatic" perspective—that is, only in a historical or legalistic spirit. Yet, what Nicholas of Cusa describes in the passage just cited is nothing else than the dialectical relationship between the one and the many, or, in terms more pertinent to our discussion, between the *primus* and the synod. "Where, therefore, is the synod, there is also primacy. And where there is primacy, there is also synod."[12]

The Phenomenon of Anti-Papism

The phenomenon of anti-papism, understood as the denial of a *primus* for the universal church and the elevation of such denial to a trait that allegedly identifies the whole Orthodox Church, is, properly speaking, heretical. In saying this, I am returning the favor, so to speak, to all those who have taken upon themselves the onerous task of defending Orthodoxy against all kinds of heresy. And heresy is all they see. Any difference, not necessarily in matters of dogma but also in liturgy, in language, in vestments, in appearance, is immediately and solemnly denounced as heresy.

Anticipating the reaction of some who may find such a statement dangerous and inflammatory, I wonder if it is possible that anti-papism could be confused with Orthodoxy. And if there is such a possibility, is it not all the more necessary and urgent that we speak against such a false identification, distinguishing the Church to which we belong and which we serve—I speak here as an Orthodox clergyman—from that party that has constructed for itself a new identity exclusively based on the hatred for the office of Peter?

Nevertheless, the phenomenon of anti-papism has become increasingly more observable within the Orthodox Church. Those who want to

11. Nicholas of Cusa, *Writings on Church and Reform*, 437.
12. Zizioulas, "Ὁ Συνοδικὸς Θεσμός," 40.

Part One—Revisiting Theological Differences

elevate their dislike for the pope into a definition for the Orthodox Church as a whole do not realize that, if they were right, their version of the Church would be reduced to little more than a religious club that can trace its origins to no earlier than the schism of 1054—a club that would owe its *raison d'être* entirely to the very opponent that it opposes. Indeed, we cannot continue to accept as "genuinely" Orthodox those things that are simply the opposite of what the Catholic Church believes. Orthodoxy cannot be merely reactionary, possessed, as it were, by the demonic spirit of naysaying, bereft of any creative powers in theology, where what constitutes "me" is always a negation of the "other."[13] *Truth, I would suggest, is antinomian and, thus, never antithetical.*[14]

For philosophy as well as for psychology, the mechanism of affirming oneself, individually or collectively, in contradistinction over and against the other is well known. In fact, the more fragile one's ideological constitution, the more necessary such a strategy is. The more similar I am to my other, the more likely it is that this constitutive hostility will become fiercer because there is a greater risk that I might be confused with this other.[15] Western cultures have perpetuated this phenomenon through various foundational myths. The ancient city of Rome, for example, was founded by means of a fratricide between Remus and Romulus. The political function of the myth, as a foundational allegory, has been recorded and one can find analogies all the way from the "sinners" and "saints" aboard the Mayflower to the fight for sovereignty between two English-speaking nations in Northern Ireland. We could, of course, recall the archetypical case of Abel's murder of Cain, paying attention to the gloss that the Scripture provides, namely that Cain, after he had killed his brother and perhaps as a result of that, went on to become the founder of the first city.

At the very least, this discussion requires that we reconsider the question of whether or not we need a *primus* in the Orthodox Church. And, if so, who or what might play such a role?

---

13. A case in point would be the Photian invention of *monopatrism* as a reaction to the *filioque*. See chapter 2, note 8 above.

14. I have in mind Pavel Florensky's excellent analysis of the antinomian character of the Christian truth, understood as the integration of antitheses, antitheses that are to be found within any dogmatic assertion. See Florensky, *The Pillar and Ground of the Truth*.

15. For a philosophical discussion of the demonization of otherness as a process of forming and affirming one's identity, see Kearney, *Strangers, Gods, and Monsters*. Of course, the dialectic of other versus same goes as far back as the Eleatic Stranger in Plato's *Sophist*.

The Need for Primacy

Concerning the question of whether the Orthodox Church needs a *primus*, and especially at the universal level, I will appeal to a personal experience. In 2005, I was given permission to attend the deliberations of the International Joint Commission on the Theological Dialogue between the two churches, which convened, after a hiatus, in Belgrade. I remember how that experience led me to the paradoxical realization that the Orthodox churches cannot unite with Rome as long as they are not united with Rome. What I mean by this paradox is that the very absence of the authority that a *primus* would have exercised at the pan-Orthodox level hinders the efforts of remedying this institutional lacuna. In other words, the fact that the Orthodox churches today refuse to recognize a Rome-like primacy among themselves becomes the major problem in their dialogue with Rome.[16]

For one of the fundamental presuppositions of any dialogue, especially a theological dialogue, is consistency. The demand for consistency is related, in my opinion, to the question of authority. Who can speak on behalf of the Orthodox Church? Who is entitled to do so? Orthodox faithful today become familiar with a phenomenon that takes alarming dimensions, namely, the rise of a movement within the Orthodox Church consisting of zealots who see themselves as the rightful "guardians of Orthodoxy," over and against the Church's institutionalized authority. In their ferocity against the Western other, these "guardians of Orthodoxy" reject any notion of primacy, espousing and promoting an ecclesiology that they misunderstand to be democratic in its structure of equality. Among their mistakes is the conflation of the ideas of conciliarity, *sobornost*, and episcopal equality. In one historian's view "all titles of precedence, including that of 'patriarch,' were common to the entire episcopate [sc., in the East]."[17] He goes on to cite

---

16. This sentiment was proven all too accurate at the next meeting of the Commission in Ravenna (2006), when the Patriarchate of Moscow decided to withdraw its representatives from the meeting in protest against the participation of the Orthodox Church of Estonia (whose autonomy, granted by the Ecumenical Patriarchate, Moscow refuses to recognize). For an account and assessment of these unfortunate events, see Nichols, *Rome and the Eastern Churches*, 368–70. On December 26, 2013, the Synod of the Patriarchate of Moscow issued a document critical of the Ravenna Statement ("Position of the Moscow Patriarchate on the Problem of Primacy in the Universal Church"). Since its publication, this decision has sparked a flurry of reactions by a number of theologians and hierarchs. The most representative response is that of Elpidophoros Lambriniadis (Metropolitan of Bursa), "First Without Equals."

17. Papadakis, *Christian East*, 309.

Part One—Revisiting Theological Differences

Nicetas of Ancyra, who wrote that "all bishops are fathers, shepherds and leaders; and it is clear that there are no special canons for metropolitans, distinct from those which apply to archbishops, or bishops. For the laying-on of hands is the same for all, and their participation in the divine liturgy is identical and all pronounce the same prayers."[18] However, there *are* canons that expressly differentiate between sees, their ranking, their privileges and prerogatives, and so on.[19] What the argument of episcopal equality fails to understand is that, even though every bishop is sacramentally equal to every other bishop, not every city is administratively equal to every other city; and therefore, *the bishop* of Rome, for example, even though in terms of priesthood he is equal to the bishop of every other city, he is yet not equal to them insofar as he is the bishop *of Rome*. Episcopal equality is a sophism, for it compares bishop to bishop without taking into consideration the city over which a bishop presides; yet it is clear that the episcopal office is not absolute, that is, it cannot exist without reference to a particular locality. Every bishop, even titular or auxiliary, is ordained as the bishop of that particular city, and it is the city that determines his ranking among other members of the episcopate.[20] Nicholas of Cusa reminds us here of the response that Pope Leo gave to Anastasius of Thessalonica: "And if ordination is general in all priest, nevertheless, [the same] rank is not shared by all, because even among the most blessed apostles, despite a similarity of honor, there was a certain distinction of power. Although all are equally chosen, nevertheless it is given to one to be preeminent over the others."[21]

18. Ibid.

19. "The sacred canons (like the 3rd canon of the Second Ecumenical Council, the 28th of the Fourth Ecumenical Council, and the 36th of the Quinisext Council) *rank* the cities, attributing to some the status of a Metropolitanate and to others the status of a Patriarchate. Among the latter, they further attribute to one primatial responsibility, to another secondary responsibility, and so on. Not all local Churches are equal, whether in order or in rank. Moreover, to the extent that a bishop is never a bishop without specific assignment but rather the presiding bishop of a local Church—that is to say, he is always the bishop of a specific city (which is an inseparable feature and condition of the episcopal ordination)—then bishops too are accordingly *ranked* (that is to say, the dignity of a Metropolis is different from that of a Patriarchate; and again, a different dignity is attributed to the ancient Patriarchates, as being endorsed by the Ecumenical Councils, and another is attributed to the modern Patriarchates). Thus, within such an order of rank, it is inconceivable that there should be no *primus*." Lambriniadis, "First Without Equals," 2.ii (emphasis in the original). On the indissoluble connection between the bishop and his diocese (whether titular or not), see Zizioulas, "Ο Συνοδικὸς Θεσμός," 13 and 27.

20. Cassidy, *Ecumenism and Interreligious Dialogue*, 12.

21. Nicholas of Cusa, *Writings on Church and Reform*, 117.

It is for this reason, too, that the protestation which one of the most distinguished Orthodox theologians of the twentieth century, Fr. Alexander Schmemann, brought forward at the end of the Second Vatican Council is ecclesiologically unfounded. According to Cardinal Cassidy, one of the objections that Fr. Schmemann raised against the Council's *Unitatis Redintegratio* was "the importance that the document gives to patriarchates, since in the Eastern tradition the patriarch does not have jurisdiction over other bishops. He is simply *primus inter pares*." On the other hand, Afanassieff and—following closely on his heels—Zizioulas find such episcopal parity unacceptable:

> In Orthodox theology, the patriarch is conceived of as being *primus inter pares* among the bishops. This formula, though generally allowed, is misleading, and it would be difficult to find justification in the history of the Orthodox Church. It is indeed doubtful that the bishops ever thought themselves the equals of the patriarch in every respect, or that he thought himself their equal. Equality is really a difficult claim, when the patriarch possesses rights of which the other bishops are deprived. . . . The patriarch as a member of the episcopate of the autocephalous church is not above it but as its leader he is the first in the episcopal body.[22]

Let me examine briefly some of the options purportedly given as the Orthodox answer to the question of authority.

The Ecumenical Council

When I was a seminarian in Athens, I was taught that, unlike the Roman Church, the highest authority in the Orthodox Church—the one authority with absolute power to decide dogmatic and canonical matters—is an interpersonal (and thus impersonal) body: the ecumenical council.[23] By

---

22. Afanassieff, "Church Which Presides in Love," 102–3. See also Vgenopoulos, *Primacy in the Church*, 131–38.

23. So Panayiotis Trempelas: ἀνωτάτη δ' ἀρχὴ τῆς καθόλου Ἐκκλησίας εἶναι ἡ Οἰκουμενικὴ Σύνοδος ("supreme authority of the universal Church is the Ecumenical Council"). Trempelas, Δογματική, 2:402. The *Dogmatic* of Christos Androutsos also agrees: ἀλλ' ἄν ὁ ἐπίσκοπος εἶνε ὁ ἀνώτατος φορεὺς τῆς ἐκκλησιαστικῆς ἐξουσίας, εἶνε φανερὸν ὅτι ἀνωτάτη ἀρχὴ τῶν μὲν ἐπὶ μέρους Ἐκκλησιῶν εἶνε ἡ σύνοδος τῶν ἐπισκόπων, πασῶν δὲ τῶν Ὀρθοδόξων Ἐκκλησιῶν τὸ σύνcλο τῶν ἐπισκόπων ("but if the bishop is the supreme bearer of ecclesiastical authority, it is evident that supreme authority of the local Churches is the synod of the bishops, while of all the Orthodox churches [the gathering of] all bishops"). Androutsos, Δογματική, 287.

asserting such a claim, the Orthodox present a not-so-implicit critique against papal primacy, which is often caricatured as a centralized, imperialistic, and therefore totalitarian and oppressive ecclesiology. In opposition to such a structure, the Orthodox take pride in what they consider a more democratic structure. They give, however, little or no thought to the fact that the synod as a manifold body presupposes the office of the One—that is, the one *primus* who, although *inter pares* as far as his sacramental faculty is concerned, remains nevertheless *unequal* in his primacy. Similarly, the patriarch or the metropolitan is also *inter pares* with the bishops who are administratively under him; yet, as the 34th Apostolic Canon makes clear, the synod cannot do anything without his consent. As the bishop is also *inter pares* with all baptized Christians, he is one of them every time he officiates—an ecclesiological truth signified by the white *sticharion* (the equivalent of the alb) that the bishop, like all clerics, wears as the first piece of his liturgical vestments. And yet, despite the fact that he is *inter pares* with the faithful (*cum fidelibus*), the local church cannot do anything without him, nor would they even exist as a community.[24]

The balanced dialectic that I have described on the universal, regional, and local levels respectively finds its articulation in the 34th Apostolic Canon mentioned earlier, which reads as follows: "The bishops of every region must acknowledge him who is first among them [*protos, primus*] and account him as their head, and do nothing of consequence without his consent; but each may do those things only which concern his own eparchy. . . . But neither let him [who is the first] do anything without the consent of the many; for so there will be unanimity, and God will be glorified through the Lord in the Holy Spirit."

There is no either/or distinction between conciliarity and primacy. No council is conceivable without a *primus*.[25] Philosophically speaking, the emphasis on primacy conforms with the idea that the "one" (in this case,

---

24. This is the ecclesiological structure reflected in such Apostolic writings as St. Ignatius of Antioch's *Letters*, in the ancient canons of the Church, like the aforementioned 34th canon of the Holy Apostles, but also, and more importantly, in ancient liturgical practices, most of them still preserved in Orthodox praxis. A now classic discussion of the role of the bishop for the local church is the doctoral dissertation of John D. Zizioulas, *Eucharist, Bishop, Church*.

25. Zizioulas, "Recent Discussions on Primacy," 242. See also Zizioulas, "Ἡ Εὐχαριστιακὴ Ἐκκλησιολογία," 23. From the Catholic perspective, see McPartlan, *Service of Love*, 41–44.

the *primus*) is both logically, ontologically, and "chronologically" prior to the "many" (the synod).

There is another reason why the ecumenical council cannot be considered an *institution of authority* for the Church—without, of course, meaning to say that ecumenical councils have no authority. The weight of the argument here falls not so much on authority but on the concept of the institution. An institution (θεσμός) implies both permanence and regularity, two basic characteristics lacking from the convocation of an ecumenical council that has more of the character of an *event* (extraordinary in nature) than that of a standing institution.[26]

Christ Himself

Another position that one hears often from the Orthodox is that the Church needs no *primus* because Christ himself is the head of the Church. But is this true exclusively on the universal level? Indeed, on both the regional and local levels, ecclesial structures presuppose that the bishop is Christ's living icon. No Orthodox would accept the claim that the bishop is not needed as head of either the diocese or the metropolitanate simply because that role is filled by Christ himself. Furthermore, such a naive assertion ignores the profound theological significance of Christ's ascension[27] and runs the risk of degenerating into some individualistic, private piety that would dispense with the ecclesial structure altogether. Apart from the Eucharist, Christ is not with us physically; otherwise, the Church's expectation of his future coming would be absurd. Moreover, saying that Christ is present in the Eucharist points to him who is physically present and who alone has the authority to celebrate the Eucharist *in persona Christi*—that is, the bishop. Again it is worth citing at length Afanassieff's elaboration of this problem:

> A single body must be crowned by a single head, showing in his own person the unity of the whole system. If we take the universal

---

26. See Zizioulas, "Ο Συνοδικὸς Θεσμός," 20–21. In agreement, the Ravenna document states that "an Ecumenical Council is not an 'institution' whose frequency can be regulated by canons; it is rather an 'event,' a *kairos* inspired by the Holy Spirit who guides the Church so as to engender within it the institutions which it needs and which respond to its nature" (cited in McPartlan, *Service of Love*, 73). See also Vgenopoulos, *Primacy in the Church*, 63 and 130. Thus, DeVille's proposal of a "permanent ecumenical synod" is unfortunate (*Orthodoxy and the Roman Papacy*, 127 and 150–55).

27. For a discussion of the bearing of the Ascension on ecclesiology, see Farrow, *Ascension and Ecclesia*.

theory of the Church, we cannot refute the doctrine of universal primacy just by saying that the Church has Christ as Head; that is an indisputable truth, and supporters of primacy do not themselves oppose it. The real question is: If the Church has an invisible head (Christ), can she, or can she not, also have a visible head? If not, then why can a local church have a single head in the person of its bishop? In other words, why can one part of the Universal Church have a single head, while the entire Universal Church is deprived of one?[28]

The Common Rule of Faith and Ritual

Even less needs to be said about the common rule of faith and ritual as a source of authority in the Church or as agents that could effect and represent the unity of the Church. Both these factors have been proven historically and practically ineffective in preserving the unity of Orthodox churches or Orthodox communities with each other. Furthermore, the multiplicity of rites within the Christian Roman Empire and the recent introduction of Western-rite communities within Orthodox jurisdictions deprive this argument of any validity.[29] A more serious consideration, however, that begins to emerge at this point is whether the office of primacy can be exercised at any level of the Church's manifestation by something *impersonal*.

Primacy Is Personal

In Christian theology *the principle of unity is always a person*. This simple truth can be attested on the Trinitarian, the christological, and the ecclesiological level, demonstrating, incidentally, the interrelated nature of these three branches of theology. The mystery of the Holy Trinity places in front of us, in an eminent way, the problematic of the dialectic between the one and the many, unity and difference, communion and otherness. It is well known that what safeguards the oneness of God and prevents faith

---

28. Afanassieff, "Church Which Presides," 99–100. See also Vgenopoulos, *Primacy in the Church*, 49.

29. To my knowledge two Orthodox churches, the Antiochean Orthodox Archdiocese of North America and the Russian Orthodox Church Outside of Russia (ROCOR), have introduced such Western-rite communities—a form of Orthodox Uniate—in the United States.

in the Holy Trinity from lapsing into tritheism is the *person* of the Father. The "monarchy of the Father" indicates clearly that the coincidence and co-affirmation of unity and plurality in the Holy Trinity is exercised by a person—the Father. As the symbol of our faith, the creed that we recite in every eucharistic gathering, attests in its first article, the *one* God we believe in is a *person*, the *Father* ("I believe in *one* God, the Father, the Almighty..."). The oneness of God is safeguarded *not* by some impersonal divine essence but by the person of the Father. Of course, any reference to the Father cannot be understood without evoking at the same time the Son, without whom the Father is not a Father. Precisely because the Father is a person, he cannot be mentioned or understood outside the relation with the other two persons of the Holy Trinity. Therefore, the monarchy of the Father should not make us fear that the person of the Father is overemphasized at the expense, perhaps, of the Trinitarian communion. Rather, it is that person, or more accurately, the personal character, that safeguards the *homoousian* community of the Holy Trinity. In a similar vein, the christological debates, which began in the fifth century, sought, again, to come to terms with the distinction between the one and the many. Here, of course, the many are the two natures of Christ, which became a cause of puzzlement, for the difficulty was the simultaneous affirmation of the perfect divinity and perfect humanity of Christ, on the one hand, and of the fact that Christ was *one*, on the other. Again, the principle of unity, a unity "without division" and "without confusion," as the definition of the Ecumenical Council of Chalcedon puts it, is safeguarded and upheld by a person—namely, the person of the incarnate Logos.[30] My argument is that there must be a consistency between these dogmatic claims and our ecclesiological model, if we do not wish to divorce ecclesiology from theology. Ecclesiologically too, then, the principle of unity for all and each of the three levels of ecclesial structure *must* be a person, a *primus*. Here, I invoke the unambiguous witness of the metropolitan Elpidophoros (Lambriniadis) of Bursa, who, as the Chief-Secretary of the Ecumenical Patriarchate, delivered an important speech at the Chapel of the Holy Cross Theological School in Brookline, saying the following:

> Let me add that the refusal to recognize primacy within the Orthodox Church, a primacy that necessarily cannot but be embodied by a *primus* (that is by a bishop who has the prerogative of being

---

30. For the capital implications of Chalcedonian Christology, see Zizioulas, *Communion and Otherness*, especially chapter 7 (250-85).

the first among his fellow bishops) constitutes nothing less than *heresy*.³¹ It cannot be accepted, as often it is said, that unity among the Orthodox Churches is safeguarded either by a common norm of faith and worship or by the Ecumenical Council as an institution. Both of these factors are impersonal while in our Orthodox theology the principle of unity is always a person. Indeed, in the level of the Holy Trinity the principle of unity is not the divine essence but the Person of the Father ("Monarchy" of the Father), at the ecclesiological level of the local Church the principle of unity is not the presbyterium or the common worship of the Christians but the person of the Bishop, so too in the Pan-Orthodox level the principle of unity cannot be an idea or an institution but it needs to be, if we are to be consistent with our theology, a person.³²

The Metropolitan of Pergamon John (Zizioulas) has devoted a number of articles to this topic (two of them recently published by Θεολογία, the official theological journal of the Holy Synod of the Church of Greece), in which he explicitly identifies primacy with a person. As he writes, "Primacy is attached to a particular office or ministry and to a particular person."³³ For Zizioulas, furthermore, church councils are an evolution of the eucharistic

---

31. This is, indeed, supported by a number of patristic texts. We mention here the most representative of them, namely, St. Cyril of Jerusalem's sermons in which "the axiom of monarchy" is explicitly identified with "the axiom of the Father's fatherhood"; St. Basil's treatise *Contra Eunomium* (especially I:20, 24, 25; II:12; III:6) and chapter 18 of his *De Spiritu Sanctu*; and in the *Theological Orations* of St. Gregory Nazianzen. For a discussion of the patristic sources on the monarchy of the Father, see Jevtić, Χριστός: Ἀρχὴ καὶ Τέλος, 222–26, as well as chapter 3 of Lossky, *Mystical Theology*. For metropolitan John of Pergamon (Zizioulas), primacy is a matter of dogma, therefore any anomaly with regard to it constitutes heresy; see Zizioulas, "Recent Discussions on Primacy," 237. Also Zizioulas, "Ὁ Συνοδικὸς Θεσμός": ὁ διαχωρισμὸς τῶν διοικητικῶν θεσμῶν τῆς Ἐκκλησίας ἀπὸ τὸ δόγμα δὲν εἶναι ἁπλῶς ἀτυχής, εἶναι καὶ ἐπικίνδυνος ("the separation of the administrative institutions of the Church from the dogma is not only unfortunate but also dangerous"), 5–6.

32. Lambriniadis, "Challenges of Orthodoxy in America and the Role of the Ecumenical Patriarchate." Full text posted on the official website of the Church of Greece. Inscribing the ecclesiological question of primacy within a Trinitarian context was also suggested by Fr. Emmanuel Clapsis, who in his treatment of the question writes, "Trinitarian ecclesiology also develops the insight that there is one Church as there is one nature in God, but the very best way to express the oneness of the Church is the communion of the many local churches" ("Papal Primacy," 127).

33. Zizioulas, "Recent Discussions on Primacy," 243.

assembly and therefore inexorably linked with the person who offers the Eucharist, namely, the bishop.[34]

Zizioulas's unique contribution to the question of primacy consists in refusing to divorce the question of primacy from theology proper, ultimately grounding ecclesiological primacy in the intratrinitarian mystery of otherness in communion. Thus he writes that the formation of the episcopal ministry is "ultimately linked with God's Trinitarian life in which the communion [κοινωνία] of the three persons becomes *unity* [ἑνότητα] only in one person, in the hypostasis of the Father."[35] It is worth quoting here Vgenopoulos's reading of Zizioulas's position, as it describes quite aptly the delicate dialectics between the one and the many, primacy and conciliarity:

> The overall context in which the relation between the primate and the synod should be placed is a trinitarian one, i.e., the communional life of the Holy Trinity. The very existence of the ministry of the primate is also a reflection of the life of the Holy Trinity, for, as we have just seen, Zizioulas says that the person through whom the communion of the Holy Trinity becomes unity is the Father. Thus, the communional configuration of the "one and the many" in the Trinity is invoked.[36]

The denial of the need for investing a particular person with the ministry of universal primacy is tantamount to the way that some Orthodox scholars (Antonios Alevizopoulos, Stergios Sakkos, et al.) have attempted to interpret the primacy of Peter in Matt 16:18–19 as referring not to Peter's person, but to his confession. We witness here the same error of de-personalization that we see in the attempts to assign primacy based on the rule of faith, the common rite, or the Ecumenical Synod, to name only a few examples. However, this is not how the Eastern Fathers understood the passage from St. Matthew's Gospel. Among the many examples we choose one, that of a letter addressed to Pope Leo by St. Theodore the Studite. St. Theodore writes,

> Because Christ the God gave to great Peter together with the keys of the kingdom the office of pastoral primacy [τῆς ποιμνιαρχίας

---

34. See Zizioulas, "Ο Συνοδικὸς Θεσμός," 12. On the connection of ministerial primacy with the Eucharist, Paul McPartlan's contribution in *A Service of Love* is of decisive importance.

35. Zizioulas, "Ο Συνοδικὸς Θεσμός," 32, emphasis in the original. See also Lambriniadis, "First Without Equals."

36. Vgenopoulos, *Primacy in the Church*, 129

ἀξίωμα], it is to Peter, that is, to his successor that it is necessary to refer whatever innovation is attempted by those who err from the truth. It is this that we, the humble and least, have been always taught by our Fathers . . .[37]

It is interesting to note in the case of this letter that St. Theodore affirms three points pertinent to our discussion: *a*) that Peter (and subsequently his successor) is given by Christ a certain primacy (ποιμνιαρχία) in accordance with Matt 16:18; *b*) that this primacy is personal, that is, exercised by a person (Peter, Peter's successor); and *c*) that this view was "always taught by our Fathers," that is, it was not a personal sentiment of St. Theodore but a perennial belief shared by the Fathers of old. The history of the first millennium leaves no room for doubting that the pope's primacy in terms of such Petrine ministry was universally acknowledged and accepted even by the Greek-speaking Church. Theologically, there is no reason why the Orthodox Church should not do the same presently.

The history of Orthodoxy's Balkanization and the present state of its diaspora make it difficult to deny that the consequences of the heresy of anti-papism—that is, the denial of a personal primacy in the universal church—have historically been linked to racism, which was condemned as a heresy in 1872 under the name of ethnophyletism. Here, racism is treated as a heresy because it ascribes the role of primacy to the nation, the "*ethnos*."[38] Thus, it commits a grave abuse of the theological principle we

---

37. Theodore the Studite, *Letter* 33 (PG 99:1017). The Greek reads as follows: Ἐπειδήπερ Πέτρῳ τῷ μεγάλῳ δέδωκε Χριστὸς ὁ Θεὸς μετὰ τὰς κλεῖς τῆς βασιλείας τῶν οὐρανῶν, καὶ τὸ τῆς ποιμνιαρχίας ἀξίωμα, πρὸς Πέτρον, ἤτοι τὸν αὐτοῦ διάδοχον, ὁτιοῦν καινοτομούμενον ἐν τῇ καθολικῇ Ἐκκλησίᾳ παρὰ τῶν ἀποσφαλλομένων τῆς ἀληθείας, ἀναγκαῖον ἀναφέρεσθαι. Τοῦτο τοιγαροῦν δεδιδαγμένοι καὶ ἡμεῖς οἱ ταπεινοὶ καὶ ἐλάχιστοι, ἐκ τῶν ἀνέκαθεν ἁγίων Πατέρων ἡμῶν . . .

38. Aidan Nichols paints a bleak picture on what he describes as "the failure of the ecumenical patriarchate to maintain at any rate an effective *analogy* with the church of Rome in [preventing the crystallization of national churches that operate as the religious arms of their *ethnos*]." One of the factors he sees as responsible for this failure "derives from the circumstance that the emancipation of the Orthodox Church in the lands of the former Ottoman Empire coincided with the arrival in those territories of the ideological packhorse of nineteenth-century nationalism. The new patriarchates of Serbia, Romania, and Bulgaria, as well as the autocephalous churches that orbit as planets these minor stars, are too firmly wedded to the national idea to be divorced therefrom at Constantinople's say-so—as the ineffective late nineteenth-century condemnation of 'Filetism' by the Phanar demonstrates." *Rome and the Eastern Churches*, 378–80. In spite of Constantinople's perceived "failure" to impose its will as the first see within the Orthodox world, a role that has been impeded by other reasons, some of which have to

have described above, by substituting the *person* of the *primus* with the impersonal collectivity of the nation, sacrificing the particular for the universal. Racism invests a penultimate category—that of race or language—with the authority of the ultimate, ignoring that such categories will be eschatologically overcome, as the experience of Pentecost both promises and anticipates. By doing so, national churches preclude the eschatological vision of the gospel by realizing it in the present through a form of confessional or ethnic triumphalism. But, at the same time, we also have the phenomenon of the self-proclaimed "guardians of Orthodoxy," who, implicitly and illicitly, assert themselves and their criteria for Orthodoxy over the entire church, as a type of primatial vision that supplants the legitimate structures of the Church (i.e., the bishop).

By entrusting the ministry of primacy to a person, the Church defends herself against the insidious danger of idolatry. Idolatry is endemic to ideology. It elevates theories, concepts, or structures (no matter how benign or well-intended) to a normative status in the Church, which, in effect, establishes ideologies. I say that with respect to those who might prefer to see in the structure of the Church a democracy that would emphasize equality among the faithful, understanding the Church primarily as a community of equal members that "co-celebrate" the Eucharist. Such views are open and susceptible to idolization. On the other hand, the person of the bishop, in his concreteness and not in spite of his shortcomings and failures but precisely *on account of them*, offers himself as an antidote to idolatry insofar as his humanity cannot but subject him to a process of demystification that would be difficult, if not impossible, to be exercised with respect to a fleshless, impersonal construction. Finally, there are those who would perhaps feel scandalized by the fact that such a role is given to mere humans. Understandable as this concern might be, we should be mindful that the origin of this scandal is to be found nowhere else but in God's incarnation. Would those who protest today that a person, namely the bishop, has come to occupy such a central position in our theologies and worship express the same protestations that a Nazarene man claimed to be "he who is"? Indeed, "blessed is he who shall not be scandalized" by the person of God (Matt 11:6; Luke 7:23). In short, what I am trying to argue is this: it is the

do with the Orthodox world's inability or unwillingness to formulate and accept such a primacy, it should be made clear that the Ecumenical Patriarchate has never relinquished its canonical duty to exercise its ministerial prerogatives as it understands them. The reign of the current Ecumenical Patriarch Bartholomew leaves no doubts of the first Throne's resoluteness to remain such.

evident weakness of the person—and especially of the person who, as the head, cannot hide—that becomes, at the same time, his secret strength. In the words of G. K. Chesterton,

> When Christ at a symbolic moment was establishing His great society, he chose for its cornerstone neither the brilliant Paul nor the mystic John, but a shuffler, a snob, a coward—in a word, a man. And upon this rock He has built His Church, and the gates of Hell have not prevailed against it. All the empires and the kingdoms have failed, because of this inherent and continual weakness, that they were founded by strong men and upon strong men. But this one thing, the historic Christian Church, was founded on a weak man, and for that reason it is indestructible. For no chain is stronger than its weakest link.[39]

The denial of the pope's primacy has created a lacuna of authority in the Orthodox Church that has resulted, on the one hand, in the endless divisions of autocephalies and autonomies with multiple canonical jurisdictions over one region and, on the other, in the rogue fanaticism of para-ecclesial groups. It remains to be seen if this situation will awaken the Orthodox world from its dogmatic slumber. I hope that our Catholic brothers and sisters will learn something from our predicament.

In the foregoing we were concerned only with the task of showing that the ministry of primacy at the universal level is, from an Orthodox point of view, as necessary for the Church as it is at the diocesan and eparchial levels. Such a ministry cannot be performed save by the person of the bishop. Reality—that is, the current state of affairs at the pan-Orthodox level—as well as the Orthodox Church's theology make it clear that neither an abstract principle nor an impersonal body can satisfactorily exercise the ministry of primacy. We have left the thorny question about the specific privileges and prerogatives into which this ministry translates untouched. This would be indeed another day's work.[40] What we can be sure of is that such primacy cannot be merely "of honor": "there can be no honour in the Church of the Servant, Jesus Christ, that is not based on service—and therefore, on ministerial function."[41] At least so much has been implied here: the *primus*

---

39. Chesterton, "Mr. Bernard Shaw," 70.

40. Adam A. J. DeVille takes up this task in his *Orthodoxy and the Roman Papacy*, 147–60.

41. Nichols, *Rome and the Eastern Churches*, 317. So too McPartlan, citing Brian Daley, in *Service of Love*, 55. Zizioulas too argues that primacy (in every level) is never merely honorific but it "involves actual duties and responsibilities" (Vgenopoulos,

offers witness to the Church's unity; he is a visible sign of such unity and the means by which that unity is universally effected and proclaimed.

We have offered these few reflections on the ministry of Petrine primacy in response to the continuous invitation of Popes John Paul II and Benedict XVI to do so. Most recently Pope Francis renewed this invitation during his address at the Church of the Holy Sepulcher as part of his apostolic pilgrimage with Ecumenical Patriarch Bartholomew in Jerusalem: "Here I reiterate the hope already expressed by my predecessors for a continued dialogue with all our brothers and sisters in Christ, aimed at finding a means of exercising the specific ministry of the Bishop of Rome which, in fidelity to his mission, can be open to a new situation and can be, in the present context, a service of love and of communion acknowledged by all."[42]

Primacy within the Orthodox World

In the foregoing part of this chapter we had the opportunity to discuss the need for primacy in the Church in general. Our discussion demonstrated, to the best of our abilities, that such a primacy is required by the very structure of the Church's ecclesiology and that, furthermore, it is a prerequisite necessitated by the Church's theology. It was that same theology that gave us the insight to primacy's personal character insofar as it can be exercised only by a person. That person is, in principle, the bishop of Rome. Yet the separation of the two churches has meant, first and foremost, that the Orthodox churches have been deprived of the benefits embodied in such a personal primacy. One might have expected that, in the absence of the Roman primacy, the see that follows after the elder Rome in the taxis of the pentarchy ought to have been given the ministry of primacy within the Orthodox Church. That is, primacy ought to be exercised by the Patriarchate of Constantinople, the New Rome, and more specifically in the person of the patriarch of Constantinople. In fact, the ancient appellation of Constantinople as New Rome would have assumed on this occasion a quasi-prophetic meaning, as it would have anticipated that this church was

---

Primacy in the Church, 67). For an informed analysis on the meaning of the contested phrase πρεσβεῖα τιμῆς (erroneously translated as "primacy of honor") used by canon 3 of Constantinople I and canon 28 of Chalcedon, see Daley, "Position and Patronage in the Early Church," and my article (in Greek) at http://www.amen.gr/article19813.

42. Francis, Address at the Ecumenical Celebration.

destined to become the Rome for the Eastern churches in the event that the communion with the elder Rome were to be severed.

So much seems to be suggested by the spirit of the canons which afforded Constantinople with prerogatives and privileges comparable only to those of Rome (cf. canon 3 of the Second Ecumenical Council and canon 28 of the Fourth Ecumenical Council). Thus, on the authority of these two Ecumenical Councils, the Church of Constantinople was granted a unique status among the remaining Eastern patriarchates (Alexandria, Antioch, and Jerusalem), as, for the first time, a see was given jurisdictional rights beyond the borders of its immediate locality.

The justification for this state of exception[43] was provided by the primacy that Constantinople already had come to exercise as the Imperial City. The codification of that primacy by the canons was simply the de jure recognition of a ministry that Constantinople had assumed de facto. In fact, the primacy of both old and new Rome stems from an understanding of apostolicity that is not essentially bound to the antiquity of the see itself. Thus, for example, Nicholas of Cusa argues that

> although many doctors write with great distinction about the supreme priesthood of Peter, how he was set over the others, nevertheless, although the Roman pontiff may hold Peter's see, his priority [*prioritas*] is not to be argued on this basis. For it is clear that the bishops succeed apostles in places where there were no apostles. Hence [apostolic] succession is not argued from the original foundation of the see.[44]

This idea, however, is today contested and has become a point of contention among the Orthodox churches, so much so that it threatens to derail their dialogue with the Catholic Church.[45] It is, therefore, both expedient and

---

43. DeVille speaks of a patriarchate that is "*sui generis* among the Eastern patriarchates" (*Orthodoxy and the Roman Papacy*, 82).

44. Nicholas of Cusa, *Writings on Church and Reform*, 127.

45. "In October 2006 [sic], the commission [on the theological dialogue between the two churches] resumed its discussions at Ravenna, though the event was marred by a 'walkout' on the part of the Moscow patriarchate's representative. Bishop Hilarion's protest was caused not for once by the wrongdoings, real or imagined, of the Catholic Church but by the presence of a delegation from the Estonian Orthodox Church, whose autocephaly, underwritten by Constantinople, is still denied in Russia. His action demonstrated, of course, the need precisely for a strong universal primacy so as to balance synodality in the Church." Nichols, *Rome and the Eastern Churches*, 368. And he continues in assessing the unfortunate incident: "The decision of the Moscow patriarchate in October 2007 to withdraw its representatives from the Ravenna meeting . . . was not

The Petrine Primacy

appropriate for our discussion in this book to raise the crucial question of primacy *within the Orthodox world itself*. For without such primacy there can be no hope for unity, and without unity the dialogue with Rome is destined to remain fragmentary, episodic, and indecisive. In fact, the question of primacy—or more accurately the lack thereof—is the sole, singular impediment to the union of the Church, for as a theoretical issue (Petrine primacy) it divides Catholics from Orthodox, while as a reality it divides the Orthodox among themselves. In the debate over primacy the Orthodox can feel the need to unite with Rome in its most palpable and tragic urgency—yet, without the recognition of *some* primacy within the Orthodox Church, the Orthdox cannot reach out to Rome, nor could Rome reach out to the Orthodox Church. In one of those ironic turns of history, it is only Rome that can help the Orthodox communion overcome its own internal divisions. The possibility of a schism among the various Orthodox churches looms as real today as ever over any reconciliatory effort with the Catholic Church; furthermore, it taints and undermines Orthodoxy's witness to the world and remains a danger to the Orthodox Church's well-being, like a ticking time bomb placed at its foundations.

Since the fall of the Byzantine Empire the vicissitudes of history have changed in unexpected ways the geopolitical map of the Orthodox world. Russia's assent to political power, first under the czardom and more recently as a Soviet superpower, created the impression, and for some the pious expectation, that the new center of Orthodoxy could and ought to be moved to Moscow. Yet, the Patriarchate of Moscow was never transnational or international. Rather, it was always bound to the history and the destiny of the Russian people. Therefore, it could not replace the Ecumenical Patriarchate, for it could never become truly ecumenical without ceasing to be itself (the Church of Russia).

On the other hand, Constantinople as the eastern Roman capital was, by its very foundation by Constantine the Great and as the capital of a truly international empire, a cosmopolitan and universalist church. Its language was Greek, the *lingua franca* of the whole Eastern Empire, but it was comprised of people of diverse nationalities, histories, and cultures. As such it was, and still remains, best suited to avert the dangers of nationalism to

---

only an irritating impediment to that dialogue; it was precisely the sort of happening that makes Catholics think the Orthodox need the pope as much as the pope needs them" (ibid., 369).

which, as the last two centuries have made painfully clear, Orthodoxy is particularly prone.

Constantinople was ecumenical, therefore, precisely because it was that particular city. In other words, it was universal because it was particular and it was particular because it was universal. Without its particularity, that is, without its embodiment in Constantinople, the Ecumenical Throne would have been an abstraction and a utopia. Without its universality, the city would have remained parochial. In the Church of Constantinople a theological principle—one that may look paradoxical in our secular eyes—is upheld: there is no true immanence (particularity) without transcendence, nor is there a genuine transcendence (universality) without immanence.

In consequence, the mission and ministry of the Church of Constantinople is precisely to preserve this paradox that recognizes in the particular the universal, in the single individual the pleroma of an incalculable plurality, in the one the dignity of the many, or indeed of all. It is on account of such theological sensitivity—as exemplified in the parable of the lost sheep, where the one is equal to the ninety-nine—that the Church of Constantinople has rejected that secular reasoning which calculates power and relevance by numbers. Often, if only implicitly, the remark has been made that other sister churches, with more numerous flocks, should be given a primacy not in line with the Orthodox Church's tradition and canonical organization (*taxis*). That would be a primacy of numbers.[46] But is such a primacy acceptable by the Church? Primacy is a *quality*—how could it, then, be decided by *quantifying* criteria? Truth does not necessarily lie in numbers, nor can it be decided on statistical accounts. The logic of the primacy of numbers is condemned by the gospel the Church preaches, and to accept that logic would render it fundamentally inconsistent with its own kerygma.

Nevertheless, even if one were willing to discard these serious objections and, in addition, if one were to discount the flock of the Church of Constantinople in Australia, the Americas, Asia, and Western Europe, are we allowed to "disenfranchise" the dead? Are we allowed to count as nothing those same believers who inhabited for centuries the lands of the

---

46. "On the contrary, in recent times, we observe the application of a novel 'primacy,' namely a 'primacy of numbers,' which those who today find fault with the canonical universal primacy of the Mother Church dogmatize about a rank that is untestified in the tradition of the Church, but rather based on the principle *ubi russicus ibi ecclesia russicae*, that is to say 'wherever there is a Russian, there too the jurisdiction of the Russian Church extends.'" Lambriniadis, "First Without Equals."

Ecumenical Throne and whom, even though they have fallen asleep, the Church continues to commemorate daily in our liturgies and prayers? Let others boast of the numbers of their living; the Church of Constantinople is proud of its dead: martyrs and saints, confessors and hierarchs, faithful of every walk of life—a cloud of *living* souls surrounds the walls of the Phanar (cf. Heb 12:1).

On this score, too, the Church of Constantinople stands with tradition and for tradition as it was once defined in the whimsical and inimitable way of G. K. Chesterton:

> Tradition may be defined as an extension of the franchise. Tradition means giving votes to the most obscure of all classes, our ancestors. It is the democracy of the dead. Tradition refuses to submit to the small and arrogant oligarchy of those who merely happen to be walking about. All democrats object to men being disqualified by the accident of birth; tradition objects to their being disqualified by the accident of death. . . . We will have the dead at our councils. The ancient Greeks voted by stones; these shall vote by tombstones.[47]

---

47. Chesterton, *Orthodoxy*, 251.

Addendum to Part One

Unitatis Redintegratio Fifty Years Later

To REVISIT THE PAST often forms and re-forms our present. It is, therefore, an essential task to reflect on the past in order that the retrospective gaze of reflection might make possible a better understanding of the present and open up the prospects of our future.

Thus, to read today, fifty years later, a document that at its time represented a move toward a new direction cannot but take the form of a reflective re-reading that evaluates not so much the text in front of us as our relation to it. Where do we stand today, both Catholics and Orthodox, in relation to the invitation issued by the Second Vatican Council through the promulgation of *Unitatis Redintegratio*?[1] It is worth noting that the document presented itself precisely as wishing "to set before all Catholics the ways and means by which they too can respond to this grace and to this divine call" (I, 1). The desire for Christian unity is here expressly understood as a "divine call"—that is, as a calling, as a vocation extended to all Christians—and, similarly, as a grace, that is, as a gift. Both—the concept of the call and of grace—require a response if they are to be answered or received, and it is this response that I am interested in evaluating here.

It is important to note that the origins of UR are not found in the Council itself but extend to some time before the Council's convocation, to the dialogue established by a group of theologians as early as 1952 under Bishop Charriére (the Catholic Conference on Ecumenical Questions). Among these theologians Fr. Karl Rahner and Fr. Yves Congar were

---

1. Henceforth abbreviated as UR. The text of the English translation may be found on the Vatican's official website (www.vatican.va).

preeminent.[2] This detail from the history of the document is important, as it demonstrates that the Church's ecumenical ministry was firmly rooted in theology proper and because it underscores the importance that such local initiatives among brothers and sisters could have for the whole Church.

The document in its prooemium puts an emphasis on the concept of grace. The desire for Christian unity is a grace. This immediately precludes any pretentions of our own will and to our own doing. Unity will not be achieved by anything we do but, as grace, it will be given from above as "every good and perfect gift" (Jas 1:17). Ours is a task of preparation in humility, of receptivity, and of gratitude (see *UR*'s emphasis on prayer and "spiritual ecumenism" in II, §7–8).

The first chapter of the document follows a tripartite structure beginning with the Eucharist at the center of the divine economy of Christ's incarnation, passion, and resurrection, followed by the office of the episcopacy as represented by "the College of the Twelve" (I, 2) with Peter as its head, and concluding with the Holy Trinity. In each level of these three parts a different kind of unity is exemplified, a unity not only in spite of difference but, more importantly, a unity in difference. It is precisely this notion that constitutes the groundbreaking novelty of *UR*: in antithesis to an understanding of unity as uniformity (illustrated by the Catholic Church's previous calls to the separated brethren to return to her fold), in *UR* the Second Vatican Council discovers, or rather recovers in the very praxis and doctrine of the Church, a different understanding of unity that does not exclude difference and formulates a notion of difference that needs to be differentiated from division. The task of the document's second chapter is to set the theoretical groundwork of such dialectical upholding of unity and difference, while the third and final chapter spells out in the concrete examples of the Eastern and Western sister churches what the previous section had described only in terms of general principles. There too we find a prophetic statement about those who, even though they are not members of the Catholic Church, nevertheless are "bearing witness to Christ, sometimes even to the shedding of their blood" (I, 4). Indeed, today's persecution of Christians in the Middle East does not distinguish between the various Christian denominations but brings all Christians to a new kind of ecumenism, to the ecumenism of suffering and to the unity of blood. As Pope Francis remarked earlier this year, "The blood of martyrs is the seed of

---

2. See Cassidy, *Ecumenism and Interreligious Dialogue*, 3–4.

unity."[3] And as Ecumenical Patriarch Bartholomew reminded us in his address to Pope Francis, "The unity that concerns us is regrettably already occurring in certain regions of the world through the blood of martyrdom."[4]

Perhaps one of the most fascinating ideas that this document sets forth is that of "a hierarchy of truths." Addressing the Catholic theologians, and after having warned against the danger of "false irenicism" (II, 11) which would have perpetuated the various divisions simply by failing to recognize them, the fathers of the Council have this to say:

> Moreover, in ecumenical dialogue, Catholic theologians standing fast by the teaching of the Church and investigating the divine mysteries with the separated brethren must proceed with love for the truth, with charity, and with humility. When comparing doctrines with one another, they should remember that in Catholic doctrine there exists a "hierarchy" of truths, since they vary in their relation to the fundamental Christian faith. (II, 11)

The idea of a "hierarchy of truths" makes one truth indispensable: if truths are to be structured in a hierarchy, then the truth of hierarchy, this very hierarchical organization of truths, must itself be a truth that ranks if not at the top of such hierarchy then at least very high up in its relation to "the fundamental Christian faith." There is a reason why I call attention to the logic of such a hierarchical organization and it should become apparent shortly.

A little later in the next section we read with reference to the Eastern churches that "this Sacred Council solemnly repeats the declaration of previous Councils and Roman Pontiffs, that for the restoration or the maintenance of unity and communion it is necessary 'to impose no burden beyond what is essential'" (III, 18).[5]

The Council's self-restraint (one could even say "self-censorship") in not imposing on the Eastern churches any demands "beyond what is

---

3. http://www.news.va/en/news/pope-francis-to-armenian-catholicos-blood-of-marty.

4. Address by His All-Holiness Ecumenical Patriarch Bartholomew to His Holiness Pope Francis during the Divine Liturgy for the Feast of St. Andrew (November 30, 2014).

5. The same sentiment was expressly voiced by Pope Francis in his address during his apostolic visit at the Ecumenical Patriarchate (November 29, 2014): "I want to assure each one of you here that, to reach the desired goal of full unity, the Catholic Church *does not intend to impose any conditions except that of the shared profession of faith*" (my emphasis). It is important to note that these remarks followed Pope Francis's acknowledgment of *UR*'s crucial role in ecumenical dialogue.

essential" should be received as a reassuring statement calming the fears, so prevalent among the Orthodox, of papal imperialism and liturgical Latinization. Yet, the way that this declaration is received depends on what the Council understands as "essential."

I would like to make the claim that these two statements—namely, the idea of a hierarchy of truths and the idea of something that remains essential to the Church as Church beyond which no further demands should be made—are indeed connected. What is essential is precisely the truth of a hierarchy on which the hierarchy of truths is based. Furthermore, it is that essential element that has been affected in the Orthodox Church as a result of her separation from Rome and that makes unity with Rome, if not impossible, at least extremely difficult. To put it in the form of a paradox: the Orthodox Church cannot recover her unity with Rome because she is not in unity with Rome or, rather, as long as she is not in unity with Rome.

What has been affected, as a result of the polemics following the severance of communion with Rome, is precisely *the truth of hierarchy*. It may sound strange to make such a claim with respect to the Orthodox Church, which, by all accounts, seems to be as hierarchical as the Roman Church almost in every level except one: that of a universal primacy. The Orthodox Church tried to fill the vacancy that the absence of the pope created by ascribing primacy to Christ himself, or to the common rule of faith and worship, or to the ecumenical council.[6] At times, isolated voices within the Orthodox Church went as far as to deny the need of primacy altogether, opting instead for a model of a pan-Orthodox federation. Yet, without primacy there is no hierarchy, for without a *primus* the subsequent ordering makes no sense. It is for this reason that I said that the truth of hierarchy has been affected in Orthodoxy today and as a result the hierarchy of truths is in disarray, as is testified by the polemical tendency to mistake and misrepresent differences in theological style as theological differences. Primacy (and hierarchy) is not, however, a characteristic of the Church's well-being—that is, it is not a luxury that the Church could do with or without—it is essential to her, that is, it pertains to her very *being*.[7] This is the essential

---

6. Each of these three positions has found its defender in the person of a nineteenth-century Greek theologian: thus Christ as the head of the Church was supported by Mesoloras, Kiriakos advocated the spiritual unity of the Church in faith and worship, and Karmiris was in favor of the ecumenical council as the embodiment of the Church's primacy. See Vgenopoulos (now Metropolitan of Selyvria), *Primacy in the Church*, 50, 52, and 63 respectively.

7. Both Alexander Schmemann and Metropolitan John of Pergamon (Zizioulas)

beyond which no further demands should be made and indeed need not be made, were we not in danger of losing it.

About ten years ago, Cardinal Cassidy, sometime president of the Pontifical Council for Promoting Christian Unity, documented how the Joint International Commission on the Theological Dialogue between the two churches had come to a halt in Baltimore in 2000 and lamented that "internal difficulties between [the Orthodox] churches" did not make the solution of that impasse any easier.[8] After a long hiatus, the dialogue of truth was at last resumed in Belgrade in 2006 with a discussion on a text on conciliarity and authority in the Church. At the core of this text, which became known as the Ravenna declaration after its adoption in 2007, lay again the question of primacy as exercised at the local, regional, and universal levels. Ironically, the very lack of such a primacy, especially at the universal level, among the various local Orthodox churches did not allow them to agree on the question of primacy. Indeed, without a Petrine primacy there can be no hope for unity, and without unity the call issued by *UR* will be left unanswered by the Orthodox Church, as she cannot speak as *one* Church, *unified* under one pastor. As we have already pointed out in the foregoing material, it is in fact the question of primacy—or more accurately the lack thereof—that is the sole, singular impediment to the union of the church.

---

agreed that primacy pertains to the Church's *esse*. See Vgenopoulos, *Primacy in the Church*, 138–40.

8. Cassidy, *Ecumenism and Interreligious Dialogue*, 55.

PART TWO

Differences in Theological Style Reconciled

FOUR

Created and Uncreated Light

Augustinian and Palamite Approaches

IN THIS CHAPTER I propose to examine a highly contentious point of disagreement between Western and Eastern theology, namely, the character and the nature of the Old Testament theophanies. I will first present the reasons that elevate such a seemingly minor point into a major theological debate between the Augustine-influenced West and the Augustine-opposing East. Then, I will try to reconcile these two theories of signification: a modern theory of sign (anticipated by Augustine) and a premodern understanding of symbol (espoused by Orthodox theology). A scholar who has made some decisive contributions toward such a possible reconciliation is Hans Urs von Balthasar (in his *Herrlichkeit*). He overcame the impasse of the pseudo-dilemma between Old Testament theophanies as either created or uncreated by developing a more nuanced theory of signification that accommodates and affirms that signs are visible manifestations of the invisible God (cf. Col 1:15) in a way that reinterprets the meaning of a sign's dual character. In following his insights, I shall suggest that the problem of the experience of God be once again situated within the christological context where it belongs.

What is at stake here is far more than a difference in biblical hermeneutics. It is the very possibility of an experience of God that both interpretations seek to safeguard. Each side, however, accuses the other of denying the possibility of an experience of God. For St. Augustine, an uncreated manifestation of God would have made little sense; as uncreated, it would

51

Part Two—Differences in Theological Style Reconciled

also have been imperceptible and that would have undermined the *reality* of the theophanic experience in his eyes. In the East, to describe theophanies as created meant that they are no longer about God but merely about creation. Furthermore, the distinction of essence/energies, central to the interpretation of the theophanic narrative promulgated by St. Gregory Palamas, grounds the entire theological character of the East, for it is upon this distinction that apophatic theology, the theology of icons and sacraments, and also the doctrine of *theosis* depend. Can these two views, and ultimately two different theologies of the experience of God, be reconciled?[1]

The Christian exegete of the Hebrew Scriptures is confronted with a difficult problem in certain passages dealing with the manifestations of God: *who*—that is, which person of the Holy Trinity—speaks and appears to Moses and Elijah on Mt. Sinai (Exod 19) or on Mt. Horeb (Exod 3 and 33; 1 Kgs 19)? Closely related to this first question (the who question) is another one: *how* does God appear in these manifestations, given the many scriptural interdictions against such an immediate vision of God (in particular, Exod 33:20)? What is at stake in those two questions is much more than a minor problem of scriptural hermeneutics—in fact, two theological principles of cardinal importance have come to depend upon the way we answer these questions. These principles, which, in my opinion, must be defended, are:

1. God can be experienced by man; that experience is described as a theophany, and

2. Such theophanic experience must also involve the human body.[2]

---

[1]. Admittedly, St. Augustine has recently become the "whipping boy" of Eastern Orthodox theologians, who like to trace in him most of what they regard as problematic in the Western theological and philosophical tradition. The works of John Romanides and Christos Yannaras are good examples of such an attitude. St. Augustine's reputation in Byzantine times was rather unquestionable. Photius cites him in his *Mystagogia* and attributes whatever errors are to be found in Augustine's works to deliberate corruption of his manuscripts by the hand of his epigones (71–72, PG 102:352–53); Mark of Ephesus (Eugenikos) also used arguments from Augustine's *Soliloquiorum* and *De Trinitate* during the deliberations of the council in Ferrara. For more, see Demacopoulos and Papanikolaou, "Augustine and the Orthodox." Finally, Reinhard Flogaus' scholarship has established that St. Gregory Palamas was himself a reader of Augustine's *De Trinitate* in the Greek translation of Maximus Planudes (ca. 1255–1305), so much so as to incorporate Augustine's analyses and language in certain passages of his *Capita 150*; see Flogaus, "Palamas and Barlaam Revisited" and "Inspiration-Exploitation-Distortion."

[2]. These two points were at stake during the Hesychast controversy of the fourteen century. See Panagiotis Christou's introduction to St. Gregory Palamas's *Triads in Defence*

Created and Uncreated Light

Theological aesthetics of both Eastern and Western Christian traditions have always affirmed these two statements despite various Platonizing attempts to sell them short by emphasizing a more "spiritual" interpretation (e.g., Origen's doctrine of the spiritual senses[3]).

In the light of the incarnation the affirmation of such statements seems rather unproblematic. Once, however, we transpose this post-incarnational understanding of revelation to a pre-incarnational setting, like the one I have set to discuss here, then the difficulties, hermeneutical and theological, of the who and the how questions of the Old Testament theophanies become pressing.

The early Fathers of the third and fourth centuries had what seemed to be a reasonable answer: they suggested that it was the Logos, the second person of the Trinity, who, on account of his future manifestation in the flesh, had also appeared in the Old Testament and spoke to and through the prophets.[4] This opinion became normative for the first theologians until St. Augustine, in his *De Trinitate*, questioned it. St. Augustine's break with the tradition was necessitated in order to defend the Logos' divinity against such subordinationist theologies that would have been ready to demote the Logos precisely on account of his visibility. Invisibility was considered an essential characteristic of the divine nature to such an extent that if the Logos were said to be somehow the "visible God" then that meant, almost by definition, that he must be not fully divine.[5] St. Augustine thinks that ul-

---

of the Saintly Hesychasts (in Gregory Palamas, Συγγράμματα, 1:321).

3. For a critique of Origen's doctrine of the spiritual senses, see my *God After Metaphysics*, 147–51.

4. Kloos, "Preparing for the Vision of God," and Edmund Hill's introduction to Augustine, *The Trinity*.

5. Augustine explicitly refers to this danger in his two letters on the question of the vision of God (Letters 147 and 148). For example, he writes that "if one says that the Son was seen by the Patriarchs so that one understands that *no one has ever seen God* was said with reference to God the Father Ambrose did not, of course, lose the chance to refute by this certain heretics, that is, the Photinians, who assign a beginning to the Son of God.... But he saw other heretics, that is, the Arians, lying in ambush to cause greater destruction. For their error undoubtedly receives support if it is believed that the nature of the Father is invisible, but that of the Son is visible" (*Letters*, 2:328–29). In Letter 148 Augustine invokes the authority of St. Athanasius of Alexandria in support of his exegesis of the OT theophanies: "When the most blessed Athanaius, the bishop of Alexandria, was opposing the Arians who say that only God the Father is invisible but think that the Son and the Holy Spirit are visible, he also defended the equal invisibility of the Trinity by the testimonies of the holy scriptures and the carefulness of his arguments. He most persistently argued that God is seen *only because of his assuming a creature*,

timately the who question is not answerable and that we cannot know with certainty whether it was only one of the persons of the Trinity manifested in these theophanies or the Trinity as a whole.[6] This uncertainty notwithstanding, however, he decides in favor of a manifestation of God that takes place *through* created signs ("per formas," "per creaturam," "significative"). It is this latter assertion that would become rather controversial for the Eastern theologian who, in considering the very same scriptural passages, finds in them support for the distinction between the unknowable and incommunicable essence of God, on the one hand, and his *uncreated* energies through which he makes himself known and even participable, on the other.

Two Questions, One Answer

As we have seen, there are two questions regarding the Old Testament theophanies: *who* and *how*. For Christians, the theophanic accounts of the Old Testament pose a puzzling question: which of the three persons of the Holy Trinity did appear to the prophets?[7] For the early Fathers (Irenaeus, Justin the Martyr, Tertullian, Hilary, and Ambrose) it was an obvious and unanimous decision: it was the second person, the Logos, who, on account of his final manifestation in flesh, appeared also in the Old Testament. According to this hermeneutical principle, the Old Testament theophanies are precursors and adumbrations of the incarnation.

---

but according to the proper character of his godhead God is absolutely invisible" (ibid., 2:355, my emphasis).

6. "Finally, to conclude: the first point we undertook to investigate in our threefold division of the field was whether it was the Father or the Son or the Holy Spirit who appeared to the fathers in those various created forms; or whether it was sometimes the Father, sometimes the Son, sometimes the Holy Spirit; or whether it was simply the one and only God, that is the trinity itself, without any distinction of persons, as it is called. An examination of what seems a sufficient number of scriptural passages, and a modest and careful consideration of the divine symbols or 'sacraments' they contain, all served to teach us, I think, one lesson; that we should not be dogmatic in deciding which person of the three appeared in any bodily form or likeness to this or that patriarch or prophet, unless the whole context of the narrative provides us with probable indications" (*The Trinity*, II.18.35).

7. All of the three persons have served as possible answers to this question. Traditionally, the Father makes himself known in the OT; for a number of church fathers it is the Son who on account of his incarnation makes himself visible, albeit in tentative form; in the Nicene-Constantinople Creed it is affirmed that the Holy Spirit "spoke through the Prophets"—does this also mean that he appeared to them?

Created and Uncreated Light

St. Augustine avoided answering the who question by focusing instead on the *how*. And for good reason. In his time, to say that the Second Person of the Trinity is somehow the "visible" hypostasis of God would be to run the risk of subordinationism, that is, of undermining his equality with a God whose invisibility was taken to be synonymous with his divinity.[8] So Augustine focuses on the how question: how did God make himself manifest to the prophets? His answer seems to imply that the divine manifestation took place by means of creaturely signs.[9] In this, Augustine follows closely the scriptural accounts, which not only insist on mentioning as a means of God's manifestations what we would call "natural" phenomena—earthquakes, fires, clouds, and the like—but also affirm the reality of these manifestations. In other words, there were not "visions," or imaginary

---

8. Cf. *The Trinity*, II.3.15 (Hill, 107) and 4.20 (Hill, 111). It is precisely such historical context that necessitates the theological development in Augustine's thought, where the OT theophanies become more than Christophanies. Such development, however, cannot, in my opinion, be so overemphasized as to be made into a "revolution" comparable to that of the Reformation that would, in turn, make St. Augustine a proto-Luther of sorts. Therefore, I cannot agree with Michel René Barnes's conclusion: "By the year 400 Augustine had come to understand that in this life we were incapable of a vision of God—that we were now incapable of direct knowledge of the truth. This discovery is, of course, dramatized in *Confessions,* and we would expect two works from the same few years in Augustine's life to offer the same conclusion. Augustine had also come to understand something else about such visions: fundamentally, there was no virtue to them; there was no salvation through them. In short, Augustine had a new understanding not simply of the (im)possibility of a vision of God in this life, but of the significance of any such vision, whether complete or incomplete: whatever joy might be experienced from the sight (or even the near-sight), there was, nonetheless, no salvation in or from that vision. Salvation came from faith" ("Visible Christ," 342). If I am reading Barnes correctly, he seems to claim that Augustine denied the vision of God *in toto*, that is, not only with regard to God's essence (since this would only state the obvious) but also with regard to any (sensuous) experience of God. Such an accusation would put Augustine at odds with both the letter and spirit of the Scriptures. Furthermore, one seems to forget that St. Augustine was above all a bishop, that is, the chief celebrant of the Eucharist and minister of the sacraments by means of which salvation is to be attained. His theology was motivated not by academic but by pastoral concerns, and therefore his remarks—pertinent today as ever—against those proud individuals "who think that they can purify themselves for contemplating God and cleaving to him by their own power and strength of character" (*De Trinitate*, IV.4.20 [167]) indeed denied any salvific efficiency to such individual visions. And rightly so, inasmuch as salvation remains a matter of participation in the Church's sacramental life. See also note 22 below.

9. In this he is, in fact, in agreement with Scripture's own self-interpretation. In the famous address to the Sanhedrin, Stephen understands the theophany of Sinai as ministered through a creature: "After forty years had passed, an *angel* appeared to Moses in the flames of a burning bush in the desert near Mount Sinai" (Acts 7:30).

apparitions, but real events with real effects that were felt in the realm of our physical world.

This last point is where Augustine's interpretation parts ways with the Eastern Fathers. The concern in the East was not so much to safeguard the reality of the Old Testament manifestations (which was never contested) but their validity as precisely *theo*phanic revelations. The Eastern theologians sought to affirm that it was indeed God who appeared to the prophets. That particular concern led them back to the who question that Augustine had avoided answering. The answer that the East has to offer us, and especially in the context of Palamite theology and its subsequent reception, is quite unexpected. It is not God the Father who appears in the Old Testament theophanies, nor is it God the Son, nor is it God the Holy Spirit, but rather the divine energies that manifest God. Now, the divine energies, being divine, are fundamentally uncreated. Here we can see the conflict between Augustinian and Palamite theology taking shape: for Augustine the means of God's manifestations is creation touched by God, for Palamas it is rather God appearing to creation. It is interesting to notice how Palamas's suggested solution, instead of solving the problem, re-produces the old dichotomy (the root of the problem) between an invisible God and his visible manifestations, by transcribing it into a new modality—that of the unknown divine essence and the knowable divine energies. By introducing the solution of divine energies the East too avoids answering the disputed who question. Or to put it better, Palamas's answer is not an answer. Here we begin to see how the two questions are interrelated and interwoven, so one cannot be answered without also answering the other. Either both are answered or none.

I would venture to suggest that there is only one answer for both questions. It is easier to start with the second question, the how question. Both Eastern and Western theologies would agree that the means by which God manifests himself are something more than the natural phenomena themselves. We often read that Augustine takes these theophanies to have happened by means of merely created "signs" or "symbols"—that the theophanic events themselves were nothing more than modulations of creation; and it would seem so with good reason, for Augustine himself employs such terminology.[10]

---

10. See, for example, creaturae modos; *per* subjectam corpoream creaturam; *per* subjectam commutabilem et visibilem creaturam; *per* similes formas . . . creaturam; *per* creaturam commutabilem; *per* illas creaturae formas.

Created and Uncreated Light

It seems, though, that part of the problem with Augustine's exegesis is that his critics read into his texts *their* distinction of created/uncreated—for the Eastern Orthodox, indeed, the fundamental distinction in most theological discourse. In doing so, however, Augustine's *creatura* becomes translated as "created." I would like to suggest, however, that his concern might not have been to clarify whether the theophanies were created or uncreated at all, but rather to affirm their reality, and therefore a translation of *creatura* that might be closer to the intentions of the bishop of Hippo would be "real"—in other words, a palpable, experienceable event that was addressed to our physical being and not only *ad mentem*.[11] Read in this way, Palamas could not agree more with Augustine. For it was precisely the reality of the theophanic experience that Barlaam had denied.[12]

One should also take into consideration the fact that Augustine must have approached this problem, as every other problem proper to the Old Testament, with an eye to his polemics against the Manicheans. Augustine may indeed try to keep at bay any notion of corporeality associated with God—this was, after all, the central point of his own struggle as a hearer of the Manicheans (*Confessions*, III.7.12). A visible manifestation of God himself might have inclined one to think of God as corporeal. The sensible thing would have been, thus, to disassociate the corporeality of those manifestations from God (by assigning them to a proxy) without, however, suggesting that corporeality as such was to be regarded as evil (another Manichean danger). It was between this rock and a hard place of Manichaeism that Augustine had to navigate.[13]

---

11. This double distinction—between real and imaginary, on the one hand, and real and physical, on the other—is not unknown to the Greek East. A sixth-century defense of the saintly apparitions (*De statu animarum post mortem*), written by a certain presbyter of the Hagia Sophia in Constantinople by the name of Eustratius, introduces the terminology of ἀληθινάς (true or real) manifestations as opposed to both φυσικάς (physical) and φανταστικάς (imaginary) (2005–20). This is a useful distinction, I think, to which I intend to return below since both the concern of our discussion here and that of Eustratius's text is similar. It is characteristic, however, that although Eustratius is employing the terminology of *energeiai*, he avoids the classification of the saintly manifestations as either created or uncreated. On Eustratius's text, see Constas, "An Apology for the Cult of Saints in Late Antiquity."

12. Chiefly in his work *On Light* (Περί οωτός); see Christou's introduction to the *Triads* in Gregory Palamas, Συγγράμματα, 1:321–23.

13. One detects this delicate operation in such passages from *De Vera Religione*: "... the ineffable mercy of God did not disdain to use rational angelic creatures to teach us by means of sounds and letters, by fire and smoke and cloudy pillar, as by visible words" (Augustine, *Earlier Writings*, 275).

Furthermore, Augustine's insistence to write "*per* creaturam" indicates, I believe, his understanding of the character of the theophany not as created but *through* the created. Of course, whatever appears through the created order cannot be itself created. The light that passes through the glass of my window cannot be of the same nature as its medium because it would never be able to go through it. Similarly, the revelation granted by God appears through the created order precisely because it is not itself created. I would even dare to say that Augustine anticipates the Palamite created/uncreated distinction. For example, we read in Book X of *De Civitate Dei* the following:

> Nor should it trouble us that, even though God is invisible, we are told that he often appeared to the patriarchs in visible form. For just as the sound by which we hear a thought which was first formulated in the silence of the mind is not the same thing as the thought itself, so the visible form in which God was seen, even though he is by nature invisible, was not the same thing as God himself. Nevertheless, *it was God himself who was seen in that bodily form, just as it is the thought itself that is heard in the sound of the voice*, and the patriarchs were not unaware that they were seeing the invisible God in a bodily form which was not itself God.[14]

Finally, what has not been emphasized sufficiently, I think, is a key term that Augustine uses at least once with regard to the theophanies: *sacramenta* (*De Trinitate*, II.35). Under the influence of the theory of signs from *De Doctrina Christiana*, we often tend to take this discussion of the *De Trinitate* as also implying a similar signification theory. Are the earthquakes, the light, the fire, and the rest signs—that is, mere signifiers of God? Augustine's answer is clearly negative. They are more than signs. They are "sacraments." As neither the oil of unction nor the water of the holy water—not to mention the bread and the wine of the Eucharist—are mere signs or symbols of God but means of God's grace, so too those theophanic phenomena of the Old Testament are neither mere signs nor symbols but efficacious *indications* in which he who is indicated makes himself present.

---

14. Augustine, *City of God*, X.13 (Babcock, 320), emphasis added.

Indication

It is necessary, therefore, to begin our examination of these theophanies by distinguishing between two distinct forms of phenomenality: *a*) signification and *b*) indication. In signification, the sign or symbol is merely a *locum tenens* of what it stands for: it is, in other words, nothing more than a *vestigium* or a trace of an absent referent. The formal relationship between signifier and signified—an arbitrary relation, as de Saussure has shown—does not implicate the latter in the former. Indication, on the other hand, not only evokes what indicates but "entangles" (*Verflechtung*) what is indicated in such a way that the suprasensible is somehow embodied in the sensible and the transcendent in the immanent. This "entanglement" is, properly speaking, a chiasmus, a crisscrossed interlacing.

We attribute that nuanced understanding of indication to phenomenology, specifically to Husserl, who first analyzed the intricacies of indication in his *Logical Investigations*,[15] and to Merleau-Ponty, who, in his unfinished work *The Visible and the Invisible*,[16] showed us the far-reaching implications of such analysis. The phenomenological concept of indication (*Anzeige*) was introduced to theological discourse by von Balthasar, whose theological aesthetics presuppose it insofar as he distinguishes between two distinct modes of sensibility, one directed at the "idolatrous" sign and the other enabled by the iconic form. The latter, when applied specifically to the Old Testament manifestations, assumes the more precise appellation of "indication" (*Anzeige*[17]). It is important to follow von Balthasar more closely in these first pages of the sixth volume of his *magnum opus*, because it is there that he offers us most succinctly an answer to the how question of the Old Testament theophanies. But first, the problem:

> But suppose that these pious attempts of humanity to penetrate into the region of the inscrutable are all pushed aside by a contrary movement whereby the Abyss and Ocean of all reality, on its own initiative, presses in upon humanity in order to disclose itself, in order to reveal itself as "what" it "is": if this *could* happen, how *would it have* to happen?[18]

---

15. Specifically the "Essence of Indication" (Husserl, *Logical Investigations*, vol. 2, part 1, sec. 2).

16. Specifically chapter 2 ("The Intertwining—The Chiasm") in Merleau-Ponty, *Visible and the Invisible*, 130–55.

17. Balthasar, *Glory of the Lord*, 4:34–35.

18. Ibid., 31, emphasis in the original.

Part Two—Differences in Theological Style Reconciled

The question seems to run into an impasse, for either such an experience would be possible, but as such it would have to take place within the limits of possibility (that is, as something sensory), or it would have to surpass these limits (by remaining suprasensible) and thus be impossible and imperceptible. The either/or of the impasse is transformed into a both/and once the theophanic event is seen through the prism of indication:

> The theophanies, of which the most important takes place on Sinai, are intended to be understood as overwhelming events in which the living God becomes present. On the one hand, they occur in such a way that the sensory sphere that belongs essentially to man is brought into play: an experience takes place whereby God is externally "seen" and "heard." On the other hand, however, the person involved clearly understands that the sensory manifestation is the *indication*, as it were a signal or a symbol, for the fact that the absolute, spiritual and invisible Mightiness is here present, comparable to the way a person catches his interlocutor's attention before he begins to speak with him.[19]

God's self-revelation neither scorns the physical world nor shatters the human senses; indeed, his revelation must involve the human body and its senses. On the other hand, what the senses experience is by no means exhausted by them but remains inexhaustible, excessive, saturated with intuition; thus man knows that he is in the presence of him who is beyond experience and comprehension and his sole experience is precisely the realization that he is not comprehending, but rather comprehended by what he seeks to comprehend (cf. Phil 3:12). It is the experience of an endless indication, that experience itself—the experience of a counter-experience—is the only indication of God, and it is made possible as experience only insofar as it is thus indicated.[20]

When God reveals himself to man, when the uncreated enters into contact with the created, that encounter can leave neither the creator nor creation unaffected. In each case a change has taken place. This change is viewed differently from each of the two sides, so to speak, of the point of contact. From the side of God, what is revealed and communicated is

---

19. Ibid., 34.

20. See Kevin Hart's introduction in Hart, *Counter-Experiences*. Augustine uses the term *indication* within the context of this question: ". . . in which the person of God himself appeared visibly—not, of course, in his own substance, which remains forever invisible to corruptible eyes, but by certain indications [*certis indiciis*] given by the creature in obedience to its creator" (*City of God*, X.15 [Babcock, 322]).

indeed God and thus uncreated, but from the side of the creation, this same revelation is manifested through and by means of the physical and the material. Every revelation—from the manifestations to the patriarchs and the prophets in the Old Testament, to the Trinitarian theophanies of the New, to the sacraments of the Church—takes place according to a Chalcedonian duality that needs, by all means and regardless of its paradoxical and antinomian character, to be maintained and upheld. Every revelation involves both orders, created and uncreated, for no revelatory event and no divine manifestation could ever surpass or overcome the incarnation.[21] To say anything less would be a form of phenomenological Arianism and thus the revelation in question would not be worth its name. On the other hand, to say anything more would amount to espousing some sort of a phenomenological monophysitism.

Does this then mean that, following Barlaam, we reject the uncreated nature of the light that the Hesychasts of the controversy by the same name had claimed to see? As St. Gregory Palamas rightly realized, Barlaam's refusal to recognize the light of mystical experience as uncreated amounts to a denial of all mystical experience *in toto*, and thus his position is ultimately a form of Arianism. On the other hand, such a mystical experience can never become completely disassociated from a physical locus, be it in the form of the medium through which the uncreated manifests itself, or through the locale at which the manifestation takes place, or the channel through which the manifestation is received. I do not know of any passage in St. Gregory's corpus where he speaks of an "uncreated" earthquake or of "uncreated" thunder with regard to the Old Testament theophanies. Instead, it is certain Neopalamite theologians who are willing to radicalize St. Gregory's theology of the uncreated energies by pushing it to the other extreme of the theological spectrum, that of a Euchitean monism that ultimately dispenses with both Christ and church.[22]

---

21. Case in point is precisely the event of Mary's annunciation. The Neopalamites, who find the employment of created order in the encounter with God rather problematic, even detestable, should explain why it is that God employed a creature, an angel, to minister to his own incarnation. If the prophets of old saw nothing less than God's uncreated energies, should not Mary, who was to become the Mother of God, have at least the same experience?

22. This is also Metropolitan John's (Zizioulas) assessment. For example: "It is at this point that I disagree with Lossky and the Neopalamites, who tend to exhaust God's soteriological work with the divine energies and undermine the involvement of the *divine persons* in salvation. Consequently, I disagree also with anyone who would interpret the Cappadocians and Palamas in the same way and draw conclusions from such an

PART TWO—DIFFERENCES IN THEOLOGICAL STYLE RECONCILED

In another sense, St. Gregory seems to go too far, when, for example, he denies that the light of the transfiguration—his favorite scriptural narrative—is sensible:

> If an irrational animal happened to be present on the mountain [Tabor], would it have sensed that light brighter than the sun? I don't think so. For the glory of the Lord that shone upon the shepherds at the nativity of Christ, it is written, was not perceived by the flocks. How is it then possible that a sensible light is not seen by the eyes of those animals that can see the sensible? If the light [on Mt. Tabor] was seen by the human sensible eyes, it was seen insofar as they exceed those of the animals. In which way do they exceed them? In what other way than by the fact that through the human eyes it is the mind that sees? If not by the sensible capacity—for then even the animals would have been able to see it—then by the intelligible capacity that comprehends through the senses; or rather not even that, for every eye, particularly those nearby, would have seen the light that was brighter than the sun. If, then, it was not seen, even through the intelligible capacity, then that light is not strictly speaking sensible. And if it is not sensible, it is eternal; for the divine light, which is also called in many passages "the glory of God," is without beginning or end. Therefore, it is not sensible [αἰσθητόν].[23]

We have to ask ourselves what the spirit of a passage like this is: does Palamas mean to say that the light of the transfiguration was imperceptible altogether and thus deny the fact that Peter, James, and John had an experience of it, or rather is he keen to show that the light that shone through Christ was not a *physical* light like that of the sun and thus uncreated? In our opinion it is rather to the physical (i.e., natural) character of that light that Palamas objects and not to its sensibility per se. Indeed, Eustratius's reading of the same passage affirms the reality of Christ's transformation as well as the apparition of Moses and Elijah so strongly that he even advises against an allegorical reading of the passage in question.[24]

One might ask: is not the sensible also therefore the physical and thus by rejecting the latter, the former is also rejected? To see why this need not

interpretation" (*Communion and Otherness*, 139 n. 80). Every experience of God that might fall under the category of theophany or epiphany does not constitute a parallel option alongside the sacraments of the Church but rather is subordinated to them as an effect to its cause.

23. Palamas, *Triads*, 1, 3, 27.
24. *De statu animarum post mortem*, 507–37 (see note 11 above).

be the case, let us ask, what do we see when we look at a van Gogh painting? First and foremost we see van Gogh's style, that is, we recognize that painting as van Gogh's work, which means that what is most visible is precisely the invisible (or the nonphysical), for the style of a painting is not itself something physical. Style—that uniqueness through which the painting presents itself—is neither the theme nor the color. It is not the brushstrokes or the lines, but something that exceeds the physical dimension of the work altogether. In fact, were we to look only at the painting as a physical object (the wood of the frame, the cloth of the canvas smeared with colors, etc.) we would render the painting as painting invisible. Let us ask by employing Palamas's terminology: is style created or uncreated?

The example of the painting showed us that the phenomenon is not a thing; it is much more than a thing. But, against a Kantian understanding that would make the phenomenon a limiting and limited experience of the thing (since things have always a noumenal, that is, an unrevealed and hidden side), phenomenology believes that things do not reserve themselves but show themselves fully—indeed, in such a way that their appearance could exceed the limits of the created.

That said, as the style of a painting is not identifiable with the painting *qua* object, similarly, style cannot exist apart from the physical dimension of the painting. Thus, a revelation, even a divine revelation, cannot bypass the sensible. It makes no sense to suppose that the creator wills to manifest himself to his creation by disregarding that very creation to which he wishes to reveal himself. If the ultimate revelation of God in Christ conceded so much so as to assume a human body, what gives us the right to entertain the possibility of a revelation that would dispense with the sensible altogether? Neither in the preset age of *homo viator* nor even in the *eschata* would God surpass the revelation of the incarnation:

> The biblical experience of God in both the Old and the New Testaments is characterised as a whole by the fact that the essentially "invisible" (John 1:18) and "unapproachable" (1 Tim 6:16) God enters the sphere of creaturely visibleness, not by means of intermediary beings, but in himself. . . . This structure of biblical revelation should neither be sold short nor overplayed. . . . It could be overplayed by the view that all that God has instituted for our salvation, culminating in his Incarnation, is in the end only something preliminary which must finally be transcended by either a mystical or an eschatologico-celestial immediacy that would surpass and make superfluous the form of salvation, or, put

concretely, the humanity of Jesus Christ. This last danger is not so far removed from the Platonising currents of Christian spirituality as one would hope or want to believe: the impulsive search for an immediate vision of God that would no longer be mediated by the Son of Man, that is, by the whole of God's form in the world is the conscious or unconscious basis for many eschatological speculations. . . . The Incarnation *is* the eschaton and, as such, is unsurpassable.[25]

Tabor: Between Sinai and Horeb

In the foregoing discussion I attempted to show how the dual character of indication answers the how question concerning the mode of the theophanies. We need to turn now to the correlative who question and see in which way indication helps us answer the identity of the person thereby revealed.

"Now, every person who reveals himself," von Balthasar writes, "by speaking and acting necessarily discloses as well something about his *nature*."[26] Like a painting, for example, which we recognize as by van Gogh or by Rembrandt not because we *see* in it the painter's essence but "something about his nature," in particular the "how" of his nature, similarly a theophany does not communicate God's essence or being but the "how" of his existence. Notice how von Balthasar grounds the act of self-revelation on one condition: personhood. "Every person" he writes, for it is only a person who can reveal himself. Self-revelation is personal, that is, it cannot be initiated except by presupposing a free agent who wills to make himself known and, secondly, it cannot be materialized unless in such a way that reveals the personal mode of being of that agent. Indeed, when God reveals himself he first and foremost reveals his personhood, that is, he reveals that he is a personal being who wills to make himself known, but he also reveals "something about his nature": not the whatness (essence) but the howness (existence), as a Trinity of persons.

However, this also lies at the root of our problem. It is precisely because God reveals himself as a community of three persons—the Father, the Son, and the Holy Spirit—that his theophanic manifestations in the Old

---

25. Balthasar, *Glory of the Lord*, 1:301–2.
26. Ibid., 6:53–54, emphasis in the original.

Testament raise the question, which person of the Holy Trinity does appear to Moses and Elijah?[27]

The answer is, in my view, to be found in a later episode from the narrative of the New Testament, and in particular the story of Christ's transfiguration—in many ways a canonical text for the Christian understanding of theophanies. The episode, as recorded by the synoptics (Matt 17; Mark 9; Luke 9), presents itself not only as a parallel to those theophanies in the Old Testament that we have been examining but as their summit and culmination. Between Mount Sinai and Mount Horeb, the evangelists of the new covenant seem to claim, stands Mount Tabor.

Christ's transfiguration on Mount Tabor is a biblical theophany, a revelation within the revelation, so to speak, where Christ the revealer reveals himself by revealing his Father and his Holy Spirit. The "folly" of the incarnation, that is, the flesh of the Nazarene man, ceases for a moment its double effect of revealing while hiding and of hiding while revealing and simply radiates with divinity. The event takes place on a mountain and thus it is made to parallel, as a *typos*, the previous theophanies on Horeb and Sinai.[28] In addition, Moses and Elijah appear, offering their witness as to the identity of the One revealed: this is the same God who appeared to the prophets and the fathers of the old covenant. The visible presence of Moses and Elijah is also indicative of Mt. Sinai (associated with Moses) and Mt. Carmel (associated with Elijah). Indeed, there is an Haggadic interpretation of Isaiah in which it is said that the Messiah will come when God brings together three mountains that demarcate not only Israel's geography but also its history: Sinai, Carmel, Tabor.[29] However, Tabor reveals not only the Messiah but God himself: God the Father (in the thunderous voice), God the Son (by the unbearable light), God the Holy Spirit (in the

---

27. I leave aside the manifestation to Abraham (Gen 18) for two reasons: *a*) in that instance the theophany does not employ some "natural" phenomena (such as earthquakes, thunder, light, and the like), and *b*) the question of identity would seem rather unproblematic, given that Abraham sees "three men" (18:2) whom he addresses as "my Lord" in the singular and who patristic exegesis has thus reasonably identified as the Three Persons of the Holy Trinity (Augustine agrees here with his predecessors, *The Trinity*, II.4.19–22 [Hill, 111–13]).

28. Other structural details follow suit: only a select few ascend the mountain (Exod 24:13–14); on their descent they are met with a crowd (Exod 32:17); God reveals himself in the cloud and the voice through the cloud (Exod 24:16; 40:34). Peter seems to have understood the event precisely in terms of Exodus, hence his response to "make three tabernacles [σκηναί]," the very term used in LXX translation of Exod 25:9.

29. *Yalkut Shimoni* on Isaiah 391.

luminous cloud). Each of the persons of the Holy Trinity manifests himself in a synecdochal way, or to use a properly Trinitarian term, perichoretically. That means that the Father and the Holy Spirit appear by means of the transformation of the Son but the sonship of the Son is witnessed by the voice of the Father and the "glory" (the cloud) of the Holy Spirit. Father and Spirit are indicated in Christ and the true identity of Christ indicated by them. One person appears (in this case the Son), but he appears in such a way that the other two persons are indicated in him. It is a special mode of appearance, for the person who appears does so, not only as himself, but also as an indication for the persons who do not, strictly speaking, appear (directly at least) and whose appearance is indicated by the revealer.

Therefore, both the how and the who questions can be answered by one and the same answer summarized under the concept of indication. To the question, "In what way does God appear in the theophanies of the Old and New Testaments?" we answer as an indication, in the very sense that we have explained at some length above. To the question, "Which of the persons of the Holy Trinity appears in such divine manifestations?" we answer that all three appear by means of indication, and insofar as each of them is indicated by the other.

To say that all three persons of the Holy Trinity appeared in the one who is both revealed and revealer (the incarnate Son) through being indicated by him does not mean that their hypostatic distinctions are somehow mitigated or conflated. On the contrary: indication preserves the distinct hypostases of the Trinity, for only if the Father is not the Son can the Son indicate the Father. Revelation cannot be ascribed as the work or the activity of one particular Person, for then only that Person woul be revealed and therefore we could not speak properly of a divine revelation anymore.[30]

---

30. In many instances throughout *De Trinitate* St. Augustine affirms that the theophanies (both in the Old Testament and the New Testament) are the inseparable work of all three Persons. See for example, Book I, 7 and Book II, 18 (both passages make a direct reference to Christ's transfiguration). The most decisive text, however, is to be found at the end of Book IV (30) where St. Augustine writes, "I will say however with absolute confidence that Father and Son and Holy Spirit, God the creator, of one and the same substance, the almighty three, act inseparably." Then, he goes on to explain that if their manifestation seems distinguishable to us, it is only because of our temporal existence ("just as our words which consist of material sounds can only name Father and Son and Holy Spirit, with their own proper intervals of time, which the syllable of each word takes up, spaced off from each other by a definite separation"). Apart from linguistic examples, St. Augustine brings his favorite example of the trichotomy between memory, understanding, and will to show that, although each appears distinct, each one involves all three. St. Gregory Palamas, as well, attributes every divine activity (and revelation as

Eschatology

An aspect of this debate that has been little accounted for, if not completely overlooked, is eschatology. For Palamas the light that shone on Mt. Tabor, the mystical experiences of the saints throughout the history of the Church, and the beatific vision of God at the eschaton are one and the same event (ἕν καὶ τὸ αὐτό).[31] Eschatology is implicated in the theophanous events in a twofold way: *proleptically* and *retrospectively*.

Our enjoyment of God's vision is a demand that both Scripture and tradition make upon theology. It is indeed our hope that at the end of times we shall see God "face to face" (1 Cor 13:12) and "as he is" (1 John 3:2); and we confess that this will happen by means of our bodies (on account of the resurrection of the body). One could object that the state of the resurrected bodies will be different from our bodies as we know them in the present.[32] Perhaps. Nevertheless, the transfigured human body, by being akin to the resurrected body, can experience and indeed *has* experienced proleptically, and also in all reality, that eschatological glory.[33] Thus Palamas's reply that the Hesychasts, through their ascesis, have strived to accomplish precisely this: the overcoming of the present limitations of the body so as to experience, as if in preview, the eschatological vision.

However, such a *pre*-eschatological vision of God is precisely made possible only retrospectively by the eschaton itself—that is, by the kingdom which is to come and yet always coming, flowing, as it were, into history. At the moment of Christ's transfiguration the eschaton is not anticipated, if by this we mean simply expected, but must rather be revealed—as if the veil of time is momentarily lifted so as to allow us to take a peek at the kingdom behind it, which we, from this side of the veil, still await, but which itself already exists and unfolds. Furthermore, this already unfolding kingdom is a reality active in our historical reality insofar as it manifests itself in such moments as the transfiguration on Mt. Tabor. Similarly, the transfiguration, in its turn, was itself retroactively reaching back in history to those

---

such) to all three Persons of the Trinity in common: "Each and every of these activities is common [κοινή] to the Father and to the Son and to the Holy Spirit and in every of these good and divine volitions it is the Father and the Son and the Holy Spirit who is the essential and life-giving and illuminating activity and power" (*One Hundred and Fifty Chapters*, 91, in Gregory Palamas, Συγγράμματα, 5:88).

31. Palamas, *Triads*, 1, 3, 43.
32. See Augustine, *City of God*, XXII.29.
33. Kallistos Ware, "The Transfiguration of the Body."

Old Testament theophanies. Palamas clearly reads in the Old Testament theophanies the *results* of Christ's transfiguration on Mt. Tabor, and he considers the latter, in turn, the result of the final and eschatological vision.[34] We need to remind ourselves here of the retrospective effects of the Incarnation that the Fathers of the second and third centuries took as the basis of their exegesis. In assuming our nature, Christ also gave us the potential of participating in his.

This holds, then, as a general principle of any theological aesthetics, of which the Old Testament theophanies cannot be an exemption: there is no revelation without a transfigurative sanctification (deification), and there is no deification without revelation.[35] The revealer always gives something of himself (more accurately: he gives himself) to those to whom he reveals himself. That was all too well known to St. Augustine, who in narrating his ecstatic *Himmelflug* in the garden of Ostia—the third and last garden that would play an eminent and highly symbolic role in his *Confessions*—describes how he ascended from "the pleasures of the body's senses" to "the whole compass of material things in their various degrees," and from there to "the heavens" and the planets until, moving ever higher, he passed from the meditation of "our own souls" to the contemplation of "that Wisdom by which all these things that we know are made, all things that ever have been and all that are yet to be." Then, suddenly, "and while we spoke of the eternal Wisdom, longing for it and straining for it with all the strength of our hearts, for one fleeting instant we reached out and touched it."[36]

---

34. Palamas, *Triads*, 3, 38, 1:449.

35. "The doctrine of the beholding and perceiving (*Wahrnehmen*) of the beautiful ('aesthetics' in the sense of the *Critique of Pure Reason*) and the doctrine of the enrapturing power of the beautiful are complementarily structured, since no one can really behold who has not also already been enraptured, and no one can be enraptured who has not already perceived." Balthasar, *Glory of the Lord*, 1:10; see also 125.

36. Augustine, *Confessions*, IX.10.24.

FIVE

Will and Grace

Augustinian and Maximian Approaches

WITHIN THE CONTROVERSY THAT ensued as a result of the Council of Chalcedon's definition of Christ as one person in two natures, united "without division and without confusion," St. Maximus the Confessor found himself confronted with the problem of the Will in a way that was perhaps unprecedented in the history of philosophy.[1] In spite of Aristotle's preliminary treatment in the *Nicomachean Ethics*, the problem of the Will was not posed as a subject that deserved its own systematic and theoretical consideration before St. Augustine, who is forced to look at the enigma of willing first in its existential intensity, as recounted by his *Confessions*, and later, in the anti-Pelagian controversy, as a theological problem that implicates the Church's doctrine on anthropology, soteriology, and the sacraments.[2]

Recent scholarship on the theology of St. Maximus traces the basic frame of the development of his thought on the subject of the Will to *Letter 2* (to John Cubicularius) and the exposition on the Our Father, to the

1. I will capitalize "Will" in this section to distinguish more clearly the noun from the future tense verb.

2. For Augustine as "the first philosopher of the Will," see the testimony of Hannah Arendt in her magisterial treatment of the philosophical history of the Will in the second volume of *The Life of the Mind*, 84–110. The same conclusion is reached by Richard Sorabji, after analyzing and acknowledging the contributions of Neo-Pythagoreans, Platonists, the Stoics, the Epicureans and Plotinus ("I have ascribed to Augustine the originality of bringing all the criteria [of the concept of the Will] together"); Sorabji, "Concept of the Will," 22. In the same essay he denies, a little hastily perhaps, that St. Maximus ought to be credited with any original contribution on the subject.

works he produced during his exile in the West, such as the *Ambigua*, the *Dispute with Pyrrhus*, and the polemical *Opuscula* written during the peak of the monothelitic controversy. It is believed that St. Maximus began with two concepts, that of will and nature, which he sometimes contrasted to each other—for nature unites while the Will divides[3]—in order to refine further his terminology as to include two conceptions of willing, one natural (θέλημα φυσικό), the other associated with one's character or person (θέλημα γνωμικό).[4] The distinction between two Wills came as a result of the dialectic between nature and Will.

The Dialectic of Nature and Will

If for Augustine, in light of his polemic against Pelagius, the problem of the Will is contrasted to that of God's grace, for Maximus the same problem is formulated primarily as a question vis-à-vis nature, for he was writing against the backdrop of the christological controversies on the two natures of the incarnate Logos. In attempting to answer the question whether the

---

3. Maximus sees the result of the human fall as manifested first and foremost in the fact that the devil "has separated us in our inclinations [κατὰ τὴν γνώμην] from God and from one another . . . [and] has divided nature at the level of mode of existence [κατὰ τὸν τρόπον], fragmenting it into a multitude of opinions and imaginations" (396 D). That separation, he now more explicitly states, was "because of man's own *will*" (κατὰ τὴν θέλησιν μέν ἰδίαν τοῦ ἀνθρώπου, 397B, my emphasis). Thus "the contention and division [of inclination: γνώμης] remains irreconcilable with nature . . . dividing nature into many parts" (400C–D). It is precisely in these terms of division and unity that the grand narrative of *Letter 2* casts itself in order to explain the scattering of man into multiplicity and God's work of gathering humanity again into the union achieved by love (PG 91, column numbers as given above; English translation in Louth, *Maximus the Confessor*, 84–93). Notice here that Maximus contrasts against nature (φύσις) interchangeably two terms that signify volition: θέλησις and γνώμη. The distinction between the two had not, by that time, yet been developed.

4. McFarland, "Naturally and by Grace." It is difficult to render Maximus's phrase θέλημα γνωμικό in English; "deliberation" (or "deliberative will") and "personal will" are approximations that could, however, create more confusion rather than clarify Maximus's phrase: in light of his emphatic position that no γνωμικό θέλημα can be found in Christ, the rendition "personal will" would seem to imply that Christ lacks a personal will, forcing us to imagine a Christ without volition. Thus, I will simply leave the Greek adjective untranslated and transliterate it as "*gnomic* will." It should also be noted that in the *Disputatio cum Pyrrho*, it is Maximus himself who criticizes the expression "*gnomic* will," suggested by the monothelyte opponent of Maximus, as "a category error," for *gnōmē* itself is a concept that implies will (θέλημα). See PG 91:308D and Watts, "Two Wills in Christ?," 468 n. 68.

Will is natural and by nature or, rather, a characteristic that emerges beyond nature, we should first establish a fourfold distinction among *a)* the agent of Will (who wills?); *b)* the object of willing (what is willed?); *c)* the manner in which one wills; and *d)* the Will itself. The faculty of Will, that is, the capacity to will, cannot but belong to human nature insofar as it is a human ability in general. Similarly, the object of Will, the goal or the aim of willing, is also determined by human nature, especially as, in its fallen condition, nature can lead us away from God's Will.[5] However, as soon as we posit the question of the "who," we are already transported beyond nature toward the particular subject, the hypostasized agent of willing, that is, to a person. The subject of Will is always a person.[6] To say, as we do, that no Will is unassumed by a hypostasis does not amount to the principle "as many Wills so many willing persons." In other words, to insist that a Will is always that of a willing person does not fall into the error of affirming two persons in Christ because of his two Wills: both Wills, divine and human, are enhypostasized in the person of Christ, for he is the willing person of both. We cannot attribute the act of willing to an impersonal entity or to an abstract concept. John Macquarrie suggests that the perplexity on this point is created by the metaphysical constitution of language itself that misleads us into (mis)taking an *abstractum* for a *concretum*. Thus he raises a legitimate objection worth quoting, even if we are not willing to follow him to the conclusions he draws as a result of this objection:

> They proceeded on the false assumption that there is a faculty or organ of the mind called the "will" which has the function of making decisions. This misleading idea may have arisen because many languages have a noun (will, *voluntas*, *thelema*, etc.) which might seem to indicate some distinct "thing-like" part of our mental or spiritual equipment. But a little reflection on the use of language shows that the "will" is nothing but the activity of willing, and this is an activity of the whole person. The will is simply the self in action.[7]

---

5. Or so it would seem. As we will see later, St. Maximus seems to argue that nature cannot move astray from what God has willed for each thing inasmuch as he is the author of that movement, and that therefore it is rather our *gnōmē* that should be held responsible for our possibility for sin. More on this below.

6. See Maximus, *Ambigua*, PG 91:1261D, as well as Zizioulas, "Person and Nature in the Theology of St Maximus the Confessor."

7. Macquarrie, *Jesus Christ in Modern Thought*, 166–67. For a discussion of Macquarrie's objection, see Watts, "Two Wills in Christ?," 455–57.

Therefore, it is only the person who wills, and the phenomenon of the Will in general becomes manifest in the "I will" that man utters. Yet, all of us humans are not identical when it comes to our Will. Even if we ascribe the same Will—both as capacity and as object—to every human being, not every human wills what he will in the same way. *How* we go about actualizing our desire is, undoubtedly, differentiated from person to person, and it is this differentiation that distinguishes us from each other. Therefore, both the subject of willing and the mode of its actualization take us beyond nature to the realm of the person. And the person is *not* his or her nature.[8]

This transition is significant, for soon it is transformed into a tension between nature and the Will. As long as we speak about nature we speak about a universal, about a whatness without consideration for whether that of which we speak exists or not. Thus, our discussion remains inherently abstract. Yet, even as such, it presupposes a familiarity with the phenomenon of the Will, without which it could not have made the Will the object of a discussion, unless it was revealed to us by existence itself. Therefore, as soon as we enter the existential field, as we are compelled to do, we no longer talk about such abstractions as the human nature, but only of particular human beings; we cannot any longer treat the Will as a universal capacity, but rather we are confronted with the enigma of the "I will" in all its dramatic intensity as it was articulated in the well-known passage from the Epistle to the Romans:

> I do not know what I do. For I don't do that which I will, but I do that which I hate. And if I do what I don't want to do, I agree that the law is good. As it is, it is no longer myself, but the sin that dwells in me who does it. I know that nothing good lives in me, that is, in my flesh. For I find the will with me, but doing what is good I find not. For what I do is not the good I want to do; no, the evil I don't want to do—this I keep on doing. Now, if I do what I don't want to do, it is no longer I, but the sin that dwells in me who does it. (7:16–20)[9]

---

8. "Now we do not identify created things with their natures; *human nature is not a man.*" Aquinas, *Summa Theologiae*, Ia, 3, 3 (my emphasis). It is of importance to recall at this point another insight of St. Thomas Aquinas: "This flesh and these bones and the properties peculiar to them belong indeed to this man, but not to his nature. An individual man then possesses something which his human nature does not, so that a man and his nature are not altogether the same thing. 'Human nature' names, in fact, the formative element in man; for what gives a thing definition is formative with respect to the matter which gives it individuality" (ibid.).

9. NIV translation, substantially revised.

It was this very passage that set St. Augustine on his long and arduous way of re-examining his anti-Manichean affirmation of free Will.[10] The agony expressed in this passage, even to the point of paroxysm, reflected best in the very syntax of the text, is indicative of the experience of finding oneself at odds with oneself. The crux of the problem lies in the second half of verse 18. We do possess the ability to will (what, confusingly, is called "free will") but already this Will is determined to do "that which I hate," that is, sin (therefore, my Will is not free after all). My inability not to sin (*non posse non peccare*) is not the result of ignorance, for I *know* the good that I want, I even *want* it, but rather of my Will's inability to execute it ("but doing what is good I find not"). The name that St. Paul gives to this inability is "sin." Here "sin" refers primarily to the cause and only subsequently to the result. It is "sin" that causes me to sin. Sin begets sin. To put it differently, if I sin, if I am able to sin at present or with regard to this or that, that is because I have already sinned. "The sin that dwells in me" already prefigures the notion of *original sin*, that is, a sin ancestral of sin, the first sin by which all subsequent sins and sinning itself was made possible.[11]

The experience, however, described by Paul in the Romans passage is the perplexity that comes when one realizes that what one supposed to be one and whole is in fact perceived by the self itself as two, as the splitting into two, *a division that continuously takes place within oneself*. We need to be careful at this point: the passage speaks at the same time of both a unity and a division within that unity. If the division was not within the unity of oneself there would have been no perplexity, indeed, no pain. It is not, in other words, a battle between two individuals that concerns us here, nor is it a battle between two distinct, separate forces or realities. Rather what we have here is a self that becomes aware of itself as that division between two qualities that are equally itself. St. Paul speaks, for example, of two laws, one seen in "his members," the other in his "mind" or "after the inward man." Both, however, are his, they are him.

How could we otherwise explain our differentiation from our Will that this passage describes, if the Will becomes one and undifferentiated with our nature? And doesn't this differentiation constitute my freedom, a

---

10. The turning point marked by Augustines answers to Ambrose's successor, Simplicianus (*Miscellany of Questions in Response to Simplician I*, 33–69).

11. One should follow this idea all the way to its fullest articulation by Kierkegaard, who, delighting as always in a good paradox, never tired of affirming that "the first sin is the sin" (*Concept of Anxiety*, 30), and "through the first sin, sin came into the world" (31), and "sin presupposes itself" (32).

freedom either *for* sin or *from* sin? Is a human person's freedom to be understood with respect to its nature, to its Will, or both? Whence is human freedom? Our experience of our fallen condition makes it hardly possible to talk of a freedom according to nature: I cannot choose to eat, since I cannot choose not to eat without suffering the consequences of my nature—there is, indeed, a certain violence in nature.[12] I can choose what to eat (relative freedom of choice), but I can also choose to abstain from food (fasting), sleep (vigil), and every other biological compulsion that my nature imposes on me. If the Will is to be understood only as a natural activity, how can I resist the compulsion of the Will itself? How can I ascend to the other's Will in saying "your Will be done"? Could a nature oppose what is natural and could nature fight against nature? Whence is the human person's freedom? On the other hand, if one is to be identified completely with one's nature, then why punish or reward one? To ascribe the Will to nature, without reference to the human person, would threaten the entire spiritual ethos of the Church.

That freedom of the Will is not a matter of deliberation or choice is explained, in terms reminiscent of St. Maximus the Confessor, by Descartes in his treatment of the Will in his fourth meditation:

> In order to be free, there is no need for me to be inclined both ways; on the contrary, the more I incline in one direction—either because I clearly understand that reasons of truth and goodness point that way, or because of a divinely produced disposition of my inmost thoughts—the freer is my choice. Neither divine grace nor natural knowledge ever diminishes freedom; on the contrary, they increase and strengthen it. But the indifference I feel when there is no reason pushing me in one direction rather than another is the lowest grade of freedom; it is evidence not of any perfection of freedom, but rather of a defect in knowledge or a kind of negation. For if I always saw clearly what was true and good, I should never have to deliberate about the right judgment or choice; in that case, although I should be wholly free, it would be impossible for me ever to be in a state of indifference.[13]

The last part of Descartes' argument is precisely what compelled St. Maximus to deny a *gnomic* Will in Christ, something that baffles his readers today, who mistakenly understand such a lack as an imperfection. For Christ

---

12. With reference to our need of the "daily bread," St Maximus speaks of "the violence of nature" (διὰ τὴν βίαν τῆς φύσεως), *Expositio Orationis Dominicae*, PG 90:904A.

13. Descartes, *Meditations on First Philosophy*, 40.

"always saw clearly what was true and good," and thus he never had "to deliberate about the right judgment or choice." While for us it is the lack of such clarity that necessitates deliberation; yet this is not a perfection of free will, as it is often misunderstood, but "the lowest grade of freedom."

Christ's salvific work, even though it can be said to have as its aim the restoration of human nature, or rather, precisely because of that aim, did not operate in accordance with our nature: from his birth to his death, Christ acts according to the freedom underscored by the Will, free from the compulsion of human nature. "The mystery of the salvation," writes St. Maximus, is brought about "by things that were willed, and not by the things found under the tyranny [of nature]."[14] Employing the language of one of Maximus' early triads—God, Nature, and World—we could say that the mystery of the incarnation was God's ruse in order to attract humanity to himself and thus away from both nature and the world. In *Letter 9* (to Thalassius), Maximus conceives motion, a subject that would become of paramount importance in the development of his thought, as bringing humanity toward one of the terms of this triad. One's movement, however, is also a change into becoming by position (θέσει) what that, to which one is attracted, is by nature (φύσει). The attractions, and the corresponding movements, are mutually exclusive: both God and the world pull humanity away from nature, and nature, in turn, as the middle term (μεθόριος) between these two extremes, allows humanity neither to (re-)turn to God, nor to descend to the world.[15] It is this conception that affords Maximus the daring conclusion that the goal of God is "to free man from both the world and nature."[16]

Therefore, the attempt to ascribe the Will in all its complexity to nature alone is a futile endeavor; since we can speak of a Will only insofar as there is a willing one, as we can speak of a human nature only insofar as there is a particular human being. By granting again priority to the essence

---

14. Βουλομένων γάρ, οὐ τυραννουμένων τὸ τῆς σωτηρίας μυστήριον. Maximus, *Expositio Orationis Dominicae*, PG 90:880B.

15. Αἱ οὖν ἀκρότητες, Θεὸν δέ φημι καὶ κόσμον, ἀλλήλων καὶ τῆς μεσότητος, λέγω δὲ τὴν φύσιν, ἀπάγειν τὸν ἄνθρωπον εἰώθασιν. Ἡ δὲ μεσότης, τούτων οὖσα μεθόριος ... οὔτε πρὸς τὸν Θεὸν αὐτὸν ἀναδραμεῖν συγχωροῦσα, καὶ πρὸς τὸν κόσμον ἀφιέναι καταπεσεῖν αἰδουμένη (PG 91:446D–48A). Later on it is the human being itself that will come to be conceived as such a middle-term; see, for example, "I realize that I am, as it were, something intermediate between God and nothingness, or between supreme being and non-being ..." (Descartes, *Meditations on First Philosophy*, Mediation 4, 38).

16. Σκοπὸς γὰρ τῷ δοτῆρι τῶν ἐντολῶν, κόσμου καὶ φύσεως ἐλευθερῶσαι τὸν ἄνθρωπον (PG 91:448C).

over the person and, therefore, sacrificing the personal characteristics of the Will, allowing it to sink back to the anonymity of nature, do we not lead theology back to its Platonic captivity from which the Greek Fathers, and especially St Maximus the Confessor, worked so hard to liberate it?[17]

The Confessor and the Confessions

Maximus's differentiation between a natural Will and what he called a *gnomic* Will has caused his readers considerable difficulty, and we will examine only an aspect of the relationship between the two in the section to follow. First of all, however, we need to ask what prompted St. Maximus to introduce that differentiation, by positing the question whether the Will is a characteristic of nature or of something that transcends the natural. This question seeks to trap us in an either/or which St. Maximus successfully and prudently avoids by distinguishing between two conceptions of the Will: one that he ascribes to the human nature as such (and, in fact, to every nature, but we limit our discussion here to humanity), and the other that he reserves for the mode according to which that nature is exercised by each particular person. That the result is a doubling of the Will should not disturb us, for by positing two Wills, and thereby the possibility of a conflict as well as an accord between the two, St. Maximus offers us the possibility of taking into account sufficiently the experience that lies behind the passage from the Epistle to the Romans cited above (7:16–20). His theory of two Wills can now account for the reality of sin as well as the possibility for salvation.

No other literary passage has illustrated the theory of two Wills more memorably than the eighth book of the *Confessions*, which narrates the famous moment of St. Augustine's conversion in the garden at Milan. Even though the question of whether St. Maximus knew of St. Augustine's work

17. There are further, particularly disturbing implications of the identification between nature and the Will. If we were to transport the discussion from anthropology to God proper, then we would be forced to accept the identity between begetting and proceeding, on the one hand, and creating, on the other, since it could be said that the Father begets the Son *voluntarily* and creates the world *naturally* (on the basis of the assumed identity between nature and the Will). Then, Arianism would be triumphant once again, since it would not be possible to distinguish between the relation of the Father and Son and the relation of the Creator and his creation, thanks to a failure in differentiating properly between Will and nature. Thus, a twofold absurdity would have to ensue: either the Son would be created or creation, as proceeding from the natural and necessary Will of God, would be uncreated.

Will and Grace

has not yet yielded any satisfactory answers, we are allowed perhaps to let the work of the bishop of Hippo shed its light on the thought of the Byzantine Confessor.[18]

In his own rendering of Rom 7:16–25, St. Augustine writes,

> To find my delight in your law as far as my inmost self was concerned was of no profit to me when a different law in my bodily members was warring against the law of my mind, imprisoning me under the law of sin which held sway in my lower self. For the law of sin is that brute force of habit whereby the mind is dragged along and held fast against its will, and deservedly so because it slipped into the habit willingly. In my wretched state, who was there to free me from this death-doomed body, save your grace through Jesus Christ our Lord?[19]

Corresponding to the two selves are an equal number of *voluntates*, two Wills fighting each other: "the old and the new, the one carnal the other spiritual—and in their struggle tore [his] soul apart."[20] Augustine's agony in what is undoubtedly his personal Gethsemane is caused by two Wills driven toward different ends—his conversion would amount to nothing less than bringing the one in agreement with the other, that is, in his Will's self-surrender to God's, in saying, like Christ, "yet not as I will, but as you will" (Matt 26:39). Had Maximus read the *Confessions*, he would have recognized that what is at stake in Augustine's struggle is not much different than what he had understood to be the case in the Lord's prayer before his passion, namely, the self-surrendering of his human Will to his Divine—so Augustine's conversion constitutes at the same time a unification of his *gnomic* Will with his natural Will as it was ordered by God and toward God.[21]

---

18. On this question, see Berthold, "Did Maximus the Confessor Know Augustine?"; and more recently, Daley, "Making a Human Will Divine."

19. Augustine, *Confessions*, VIII.5.12 (Boulding, 194). Pauline terminology suggesting a rebellion of bodily members and "the law of sin in my members" is particularly apt here, given Augustine's struggle against habits formed by a licentious sexuality.

20. Ibid., VIII.5.10 (Boulding, 193).

21. For the Maximian reading of Matt 26:39, see *Opusculum 6*, PG 91:65A–68D (*On the Cosmic Mystery*, 173–76); *Opusculum 7*, PG 91:69B–89B (Louth, *Maximus the Confessor*, 180–91); and Léthel, *Théologie de l'agonie du Christ*. Of key importance here also is the following passage from *Ambiguum 7* (PG 91:1076a–b): "And this will take place because that which is within our power, I mean our free will—through which death made its entry among us, and confirmed at our expense the power of corruption—will have surrendered voluntarily and wholly to God, and perfectly subjected itself to His rule, by eliminating any wish that might contravene His will. And this is precisely why

Part Two—Differences in Theological Style Reconciled

Yet please note that this unification, if it is to be achieved, can be brought about only by the *gnomic* Will.[22] That there are *not* two natures here at war, an evil one against a good one, is made emphatically clear in *Confessions* VIII.10.22. For Augustine, ever conscious of the lurking dangers of Manichaeism, the natural capacity to will, though tainted by Adam's sin, could not be anything else but good. The Will's resistance to itself and its subsequent splitting into two opposing Wills—this monstrosity (*hoc monstrum*, repeated four times in the space of a short paragraph)—is only the result of a Will that, bedazzled by its own alleged freedom, the *posse peccare* of the second book's Edenesque garden of stolen pears, moved steadily away from God and, at the same time, away from its own nature.

In the dramatic description of the two Wills, Augustine succeeded in remaining faithful to his own (as much as the universally human) experience of sin while avoiding the Manichean temptation of justifying evil by positing an evil God. Similarly, I would like to argue, Maximus's theory of two Wills exculpates human nature, and together with it the natural Will, from any Origenist views that would deem what is created as ontologically and morally inferior.[23] (It can be argued that Maximus uses the name of

---

the Savior, exemplifying within Himself our condition, says to the Father: *Yet not as I will, but as thou wilt*" (Maximus, *Ambigua*, 1:89). St Augustine, too, saw in Christ's agony in Gethsemane the prefiguration and inclusion of all those Christians who would strive to unite the two Wills, so in *Enarrationes in Psalmos* 93.19 he writes, "How did our Lord marry two wills so that they become one in the humanity he bore? In his body, the Church, there would be some people who, after wanting to do their own will, would later follow the will of God. The Lord prefigured these people in himself. He wanted to show that, though they are weak, they still belong to him, and so he represented them in advance in his own person. He sweated blood from his whole body, as a sign that the blood of martyrs would gush from his body, the Church. . . . He revealed the human will that was in him, but if he had continued to insist on that will, he would have seemed to display perversity of heart. If you recognize that he has had compassion on you, and is setting you free in himself, imitate the next prayer he made: 'Yet not what I will, but what you will be done, Father'" (*Expositions of the Psalms*, 395).

22. Who man ultimately becomes (i.e., a man according to the flesh, the soul, or the spirit) is the result of the "direction" toward which man chooses to move (i.e., the world, nature, or God respectively): πρός τινα τούτων κινηθῇ κατὰ γνώμην ἐνδιαθέτως ὁ ἄνθρωπος (*Letter 9*, PG 91:448A). Already in *Letter 2* it is said that the law of nature will be renewed γνωμικῶς (PG 91:396D). The same idea runs through the mature works of St. Maximus; so, for example, in *Ambiguum 7* the willful surrender of the Will, after the model of Christ's prayer in Matt 26:39, is called ἐκχώρησιν γνωμικήν (PG 91:1076B).

23. This hypothesis is validated by von Balthasar's reading of Maximus's "critique of Origenism" (see his *Cosmic Liturgy*, 127–36). "While motion, for Origen, rested completely on the creature's undetermined freedom of will, and while this freedom, due to its

Mani as cryptic allusion to Origen—whom he mentions by name only once).[24] The connection becomes apparent when we are reminded that, for Maximus, the Will is defined as a natural "power" (δύναμις),[25] and power is a form of motion (κίνησις).[26] It has been argued that Maximus's recognition of a natural Will aimed at the affirmation of freedom's universality, safeguarding that every human, by participation in human nature, will equally participate in the natural gift of αὐτεξούσιον (self-determination).[27] This is as good as any speculation on the subject. What seems to be even more to the point, however, is the fact that, for Maximus, the Will and, more specifically, self-determination is a movement, indeed self-motion,[28] and as such, it needs to be interpreted within the broader context of Maximus' thought on motion. Only then will the Maximian understanding of the Will be seen in its broader cosmological implications and thus freed from its confinement in moralistic interpretations of volition.

It is well known that *Ambiguum 7* provided Fr. Polycarp Sherwood with all the necessary material that enabled him to reconstruct the Maximian refutation of Origenism.[29] That refutation's main argument, according to Sherwood's pioneering work, was "grounded in the doctrine of motion."[30] Maximus's positive reevaluation of motion turned becoming, *genesis*, and, by extension, history into instruments of teleological perfection which, in

---

extreme instability, was doomed to plunge the creature sooner or later into sin, motion for Maximus is fundamentally an orientation of nature, *which as such is good*" (130, my emphasis). Maximus constantly reminds us that God is the creator of our nature (see, for example, *Letter 2*, PG 91:397B and 404B), the giver of our being, the originator of our motion (e.g., *Ambiguum 7*, PG 91:1076B), and so on, and therefore, nature, being, and motion are as such good.

24. In Maximus, *Relatio motionis* 5–120AB; see Sherwood, *Earlier Ambigua*, 72. For examples of Maximus's references to Mani, see PG 91:28B and 40C.

25. Maximus, *Opusculum 16*, PG 91:185D and 192B.

26. ... δύναμιν δὲ, καθ' ἣν ἔχομεν τὴν τοῦ δύνασθαι κίνησιν. Maximus, *Opusculum 1*, PG 91:23B. Κίνησις and δύναμις being corresponding terms in the Maximian triads γένεσις, κίνησις, στάσις and οὐσία, δύναμις, ἐνέργεια; cf. Sherwood, *Earlier Ambigua*, 109. To which one could add, in light of *Opus. 1*, the triad φύσις, θέλησις, πρᾶξις.

27. "The choice of the category of 'nature' by Maximus as the soil of human freedom (and will) was due precisely to the intention on his part to stress that *no human being is exempt from freedom*. Only a universal abstract, such as 'nature,' could in St. Maximus' mind express this universality." Zizioulas, "Person and Nature," emphasis in the original.

28. ... αὐτοκίνητον καὶ ἀδέσποτον δύναμιν. Maximus, *Ambiguum 42*, PG90:1345D.

29. Sherwood, *The Earlier Ambigua*.

30. Ibid., 92.

the theological language of St. Maximus, translates more specifically into human salvation and deification. From the outset of this text, Maximus sets with the force of a metaphysical principle the fact that everything that moves does so as enabled by the power (δύναμιν) of its movement (κινήσεως) that is according to its desire (κατ'ἔφεσιν). This is a circumlocution to say that everything that is moved, is moved by a desire seeking its fulfillment in the desideratum (ὀρεκτόν) that has been set by its nature, while linking together Will and motion. That history is still in progress is, for Maximus, evidence that things have not yet reached the fulfillment of their desire.[31] A little later, St. Maximus will clarify that to be created amounts to being moved and to be given being implies also the gift of motion. Thus,

> If, then, rational creatures are created beings, then surely they are subject to motion, since they are moved from their natural [κατὰ φύσιν] beginning in being, toward a voluntary [κατὰ γνώμην] end in well-being.[32]

Implied here are the three steps of one of Maximus's famous triads, namely: being, well-being, ever-well-being. The first and the last of this trinity of concepts are given only by God, since they *are* God: "For the end of the motion of things that are moved is to rest within eternal well-being itself, just as their beginning was being itself, which is God, who is the giver of being and the bestower of the grace of well-being, for He is the *beginning and the end*."[33] The middle term, however, that is, "voluntary motion," depends upon us. In von Balthasar's words, motion "consists in allowing oneself to be carried by another in the depths of one's being and to be borne toward the ocean of God's rest."[34] And yet so much is at stake in this "allowing"—the whole drama of the Will is condensed here, so much so that it might give the false impression of an almost effortless abandonment to the vagaries of history. On the contrary, "to be carried by another in the depths of one's being" consists in a lifelong struggle punctuated with moments of dramatic anxiety, the kind which St. Augustine often describes in his *Confessions* and of which the Lord's agony in the Garden of his Passion was both the exemplar and recapitulation.

It is at this point that one can properly evaluate St. Maximuss' distinction between a natural and a *gnomic* Will. For by positing the *gnomic* Will

---

31. Maximus, *Ambiguum 7*, PG 91:1069B and 1072C.
32. Ibid., 1073C (translation by Constas, *The Ambigua*, 1:87).
33. Ibid., emphasis in the original.
34. Balthasar, *Cosmic Liturgy*, 130.

as distinct from natural Will, Maximus did not divorce the person's Will from its nature, nor did he allow the anonymity of nature to engulf the precious particularity that the gospel had set higher than the abstractions of the academy, but he struck a balance between the existential experience of evil and the metaphysical goodness of the creation; he affirmed motion's teleological perfection without denying human freedom from the blindness of necessity; he acknowledged human fallibility, yet he upheld our ability to receive God's grace and to accept the divine invitation to salvation; he admitted the premises of *apocatastasis* without the obligation to follow its conclusion, for "since nature and person are not identical, the restoration of nature does not of necessity entail the complete restoration of every person."[35]

In the space, the *diastema*, between protological being and eschatological ever-well-being, we find ourselves in the field where history, our history, is decided. This is the space of time, the time of action as well as of reflection, a reflection that is possible only thanks to our opening to time. However, "man is not just temporal; he *is* Time."[36] To say this is only another way of saying what Augustine had already discovered in the eleventh book of the *Confessions*, namely, that time is a property of humanity in its capacity to remember (past), to attend (present), and to expect (future). Those three ecstasies of time, as Heidegger would later call them, form another Augustinian trinity, that of being, knowledge, and will. Their parallelism would reveal the correspondence of past with being, of present with knowledge, and of the future with the Will. It is on this point that the thought of the two church fathers converges most decisively. For the refutation of Manichaeism (for Augustine) or of Origenism (for Maximus) had made it necessary to dispel the Greek cyclical notion of time by offering a corrective in the form of a new conception—rectilinear and dynamic—of history. The difference between these two theories of time is ultimately the Will. For a cyclical notion of history is bereft of a true future, and without a future the "I will" of the Will makes little sense.

Therefore, Maximus's cosmological principle expressed in the triad coming-to-being, motion, and coming-to-rest finds its application and mirror image on the personal level as well, where the Will is the motion that moves human nature, "whose origin is *before* the creature's own being

---

35. Sherwood, *Earlier Ambigua*, 204.
36. Arendt, *Life of the Mind*, vol. 2, *Willing*, 42.

and whose goal is *beyond* it,"[37] to that rest which only the alignment of the human Will with the divine Will could provide. Moreover, as in his cosmological view, rest is not simply the cessation of motion but, in fact, its intensification, so with the human Will whose willful self-surrender to God's Will finds its fulfillment, a fulfillment that will never know any satiety. The connection between the cosmological and the personal view, the connection between the human person and the cosmos, or better yet, the overlapping symmetry between History (from creation to the eschaton) and the personal history of each one of us, is the idea that provides the *Confessions* with its structure and thematic unity.[38]

The Eschatological Destiny of the Will

The crucial question, however, in my opinion, concerns the eschatological destiny of the *gnomic* Will—that is, whether the Will in general, and *gnomic* Will in particular, will in some form, however transformed or "glorified," survive at the eschaton. Will or will not the creaturely character of the creature abide eschatologically?[39] That is, does the created/uncreated distinction still hold at the end of times and in God's kingdom? If we want

---

37. Balthasar, *Cosmic Liturgy*, 145, emphasis in the original.

38. I plan to deal elsewhere in more detail with this topic. For now it should suffice to point to the three gardens of the *Confessions* as demarcating the movement from Eden (Book II) to Gethsemane (Book VIII) to Paradise (Book IX). Between the first two gardens, precisely in the middle of the narration that stretches from Book I to Book IX, that is, in the middle of Book V, Augustine, like the old Israel, crosses over the waters of the Mediterranean on his personal exodus from the land of his captivity to sin (Africa) to the promised land of his salvation through baptism (Italy). Thus, the story of humanity's falling away from God and its return to God is told again in and through the details of Augustine's personal history. When the *Confessions* begin again, in Book XI, by rehearsing the beginnings of Books I and II, the vision that propels Augustine is again that of History, from creation ("from the beginning when you made heaven and earth") to eschatological re-creation ("to that everlasting reign when we shall be with you in your holy city") (XI.2.3.) Again this trajectory is understood in terms of his own movement from being to well-being ("you . . . have granted me first to exist, that I may enjoy well-being," XIII.1.1. [Boulding, 408]).

39. "Will, therefore, man cease being a creature at the eschaton?" This is the question that Metropolitan John (Zizioulas) raises in a recent article ("Ἐσχατολογία καὶ Ὕπαρξη," 63). We shall discuss his answer below. St. Augustine's answer, on the other hand, to this same question is unambiguous: "we must admit further that even when we are like him, when we shall see him as he is—that not even then shall we be equal to him in nature. The nature that has been made is always less than the one that made it" (*The Trinity*, XV.4.26 [Hill, 417]).

the Chalcedonean formula to express an eternal truth, that is, if we want Christ to be such an eternal truth, then it must. And it must because without the hypostatic union between the uncreated divine nature and the created human nature Christ is not Christ anymore. As long as there is Christ the creation itself, and thus the created/uncreated distinction, cannot be abolished.[40]

Depending on how one is prepared to answer the questions we posed above, it can be safely predicted what view one would take with regard to the *gnomic* Will: if the created/uncreated distinction will be abolished for the sake of some eschatological panentheism (cf. 1 Cor 15:28), then *gnōmē* and the person are obstacles in this process of deification and they too must be overcome. If, on the other hand, the distinction somehow still remains, then one cannot dispense with *gnōmē*.

In the Christian East there has always been an emphasis on a strong understanding of deification—but such deification is by grace and not by nature.[41] Yet, does such a strong understanding of the deification of nature mean, in light of the created/uncreated distinction, that human nature, as deified, is eschatologically overcome not only in its fallen, but also in its creaturely character? I would opt for saying that the human nature is perfected, even though its creaturely character remains.

That nature as created *by God* is susceptible to such deification (*capax Dei*) is, of course, without question. Yet, as *created* by God it is also subject to limitations that make it impossible for it to reach such a goal by itself—naturally—otherwise we are confronted with the dangers of Pelagianism. As created by God, nature has been given both a direction as well as the impetus that will carry it toward such a goal. It is we, I admit, with our

40. On the Chalcedonean dialectic between created and uncreated, see Zizioulas, *Communion and Otherness*, especially chapter 7, 250–85. In discussing the relationship of the Will to nature we cannot lose sight of these two categories (i.e., the created and the uncreated), because the human nature as created does imply constraint and limitation—characteristics of which the divine nature is free—and therefore one should carefully avoid falling prey to speaking univocally of God's and man's nature, as is often the case in the monothelitic debates.

41. In a number of passages St. Maximus insists that deification (i.e., salvation, grace) is not within our power, nor can it be brought about by anything we do. "We experience divinization passively—we do not achieve it ourselves, because it lies beyond nature. For we have, within our nature, no power capable of receiving divinization." *Questiones ad Thalassium* 22 (PG 90:324A), as quoted in Balthasar, *Cosmic Liturgy*, 149. This is a lesson that needs to be remembered by those who are all too keen to offer in various spiritual manuals the steps ("purification-enlightenment-theosis") of a self-made deification, which is nothing else but the deception of self-idolatry.

gnomic Wills that keep taking detours away from that aim, delaying the process of our salvation—yet, I would also say that these long detours and the resistance that they represent on our part against God's plan are somehow instrumental to our salvation and that, therefore, not only would our *gnōmē* not be abolished, but even its history, which is nothing other than History itself, must be upheld and preserved.

God, I assume, does not want to save us from history—by some Neoplatonist *epistrophe* to the One—but to save our history, especially because, since the Incarnation, it has also been *his* history. If this is, indeed, a fundamental tenet of Christian faith, then God does not come into history in order to save the human nature, but rather in order to save us *from* the anonymity of our nature; a freedom not so much *from* nature itself, but rather a freedom *for* nature to leave behind the shackles of self-love (φιλαυτία) for the sake of relating through love with the other and with God.[42]

It is important to raise the seemingly obvious question, what is saved? If God does not save the human person but the human nature as a genus and as an abstraction, then he is not anymore the God "of Abraham, and of Isaac, and of Jacob" but the God of the Platonic Ideas. Another way to say this would be to ask, what has fallen—the human nature or the human person? Both questions, however, operate on an unnecessary and superficial distinction, for it is obvious that it is the human nature that is restored by the salvation of the person, as it was the human nature that had fallen by the sin of a man. It is at this point that one can fully appreciate the false dichotomies to which the separation of nature from person and of person from nature would inevitably lead.

Since for St. Maximus the *logos* of nature is the principle of unity, while the Will, and especially what he later called *gnomic* Will, is an element of differentiation, distinction, and even division, his eschatological vision of a humanity united, not only with itself, but also with God, seems to suggest the eradication of *gnomic* Will or, at the very least, its complete appropriation by nature. So, in his *Letter 2*, he speaks of *one* nature and *one* Will "with God and with one another"—a goal that will be achieved when love persuades *gnōmē* "to follow nature and not in any way to be at variance with the *logos* of nature."[43] It was passages like this one that prompted

---

42. I remind us again of Maximus's bold assertion that the goal of God is "to free man from both the world and nature" (*Letter 9*, PG 91:448C).

43. Maximus, *Letter 2*, PG 91:396C; English translation in Louth, *Maximus the Confessor*, 86–87. The same unity of the Wills is implied as the effect of the Lord's passion: "[He] made peace and reconciled us with the Father and each other through himself, by

Lars Thunberg to observe that "one might get the impression that Maximus was arguing in favour of the idea that the human will should in the end be entirely swallowed up by the divine will."[44] How can we, from within the theological vision of St. Maximus, maintain a balance between unity and difference, between natural communion and personal otherness?

In St Maximus' theology of two Wills a fundamental experience is reflected, namely, the experience of a duality that abides between *what* I am, my nature, and *who* I am, my personhood. Between the "what" (λόγος τῆς φύσεως) and the "who" or the "how" (τρόπος τῆς ὑπάρξεως) one should come to recognize what is most abstract and that which is most concrete. In each one of us two absolutes come together—the universality of nature and the particularity of personhood. Insofar as I am a human being I am no-one and everyone. Everyone, because nature is common, consubstantially common with the humankind, yet no-one, for humanity cannot assume the position implied and necessitated for the one who speaks in the first person. On the other hand, as a person I am irreducibly myself—a position uniquely posited and irreplaceable. Between these two absolutes there is a dialectic relation: if I am myself it is only insofar as I am a human being, an instantiation of the human nature; conversely, if there is a human nature, if one can think and speak of such an abstraction, that is only because of particular persons, otherwise "human nature" would have been an empty concept. The idea of a dialectical relation between nature and self might suggest certain symmetry. Yet, the person not only enjoins an ontological precedence over the community of nature, even though, in turn, it is constituted by such a community, it is also always more than its nature; the person is the surplus of an existence that refuses to be completely identified with its essence.

The *distance* of which we get a glimpse through the ontological difference between existence and existents, the distance between myself and my nature, becomes diminished in those moments where I act only naturally—when I am absorbed to the natural mandates of eating, sleeping, etc.[45] In

---

not having anymore the *gnōmē* resisting the *logos* of nature, but as [he had] the nature, so [he had] the *gnōmē* invariable." *Expositio Orationis Dominicae*, PG 90:880A. It is important to notice that here St. Maximus ascribes a *gnōmē* to Christ, a position that later, during the monothelitic polemics, he retracted (see *Disputatio cum Pyrrho*, PG 91:308D).

44. Thunberg, *Microcosm and Mediator*, 228.

45. The distance between existence and existents is best articulated and discussed by Emmanuel Levinas in one of his early works that bears this title (*Existence and Existents*, or as the French original better suggests, "from Existence to Existents"). It is there that

such moments, life becomes effortless or light as in Kundera's *Unbearable Lightness of Being*. Incidentally, but not accidentally, these are also the same moments where one becomes less personal and, one could argue, less human. On the other hand, being oneself becomes invariably a burden that needs to be taken up as one takes up his cross.[46] Being a person—personal being—constitutes and is constituted always by an agony.[47] It is not accidental that St. Maximus' discussion of such a personal will turns always to the exemplar of Christ's agony at the Garden of Gethsemane.[48]

Is the human being meant—either in its alleged prelapsarian Paradise or in the eschatological perfection—to be only a *natural* being, and if so, can we still speak of humans as distinct from animals? Is not the fall precisely this: the fall from the animal state, or the fall of the animal to humanity, where the sting of consciousness is felt at the moment when "their eyes were opened, and they realized they were naked" (Gen 3:7)? Is humanity, the very consciousness whose inception is heralded by the realization of our nakedness, the result of sin or is sin a possibility only for such a naked and fallen being? Are we to lament or perhaps rejoice over this *felix culpa* that gave humanity to man even before it gave humanity to God? And is not this ability to see myself and my sin, the ability to reflect on my sinfulness, the very occasion that sets me on the path to repentance and thus to the ultimate undoing of sin?[49] My ability to *see myself*—the ability to turn my reflective gaze upon myself—as signaled by the verse already quoted from Genesis, points at the distance of myself from myself, the distance between the I and the nature that continuously claims it for itself: that is, to the advent of consciousness. The distance that consciousness *is* appears now as an essential and fundamental human characteristic, so much so that

---

Levinas employs for the first time the term *hypostasis* in order to name the personal existent in contradistinction to impersonal existence, which has been known ever since as *il y a*.

46. "The being that is taken up [enhypostasized and made personal] is a burden." Levinas, *Existence and Existents*, 78.

47. Contemporary philosophy provides here an abundance of testimonials, from Kierkegaard's anxiety in the moment of decision (taken up again later by Heidegger in his essay "What is Metaphysics?") to Heidegger's care (*Sorge*) in *Being and Time*.

48. See, in particular, *Opuscula 6* and *7* (PG 91:65A–89B); *Opusculum 15* (Spiritual and dogmatic tome against Heraclitus's *Ekthesis*), PG 91:153–84. See also note 21 above.

49. On reflection, made possible by the distance in time, as the means of un-doing sin, see my reading of *Oedipus Rex* in Manoussakis, "Thebes Revisited."

one could not do away with it without, at the same time, getting rid of the human person as such.

Thus, our initial question about the eschatological survival of the creature's creaturely character needs now to be re-posited more specifically with reference to consciousness. Will there be a consciousness at the eschaton, that is, will time as *distentio ipsius animi* continue to characterize our existence in God's kingdom or are we to assume that we will be "like the angels in heaven" (Matt 22:30; Mark 12:25)? We know relatively little about angels in order to take their existence as a model of our life after the common resurrection.[50] Yet, they seem to be a reasonable example insofar as they are, like us, created beings, though, unlike us, they do not suffer the vicissitudes of time. I appeal one more time to St. Augustine's authority, for whom an angel

> shows no trace of mutability at any point, for it is bound fast by the whole strength of its love to you, who are always present to it; and having nothing to expect in the future, nor any memories to relegate to the past, it is neither affected by change nor a prey to distended consciousness [*nec in tempore ulla distenditur*].[51]

The opinion that humanity eschatologically will be without memory, and therefore without consciousness, would seem to find Metropolitan John (Zizioulas) in agreement. In his article "Ἐσχατολογία καὶ Ὕπαρξη" ("Eschatology and Existence"), he argues that at the eschaton the soul will not retain its ability to remember.[52] Is this loss of memory restricted to the memory of sins only, or does it concern every memory in general? On the other hand, the eschatological parables of the gospel (e.g., Luke 16:19–31) seem to suggest the preservation of memory. The rich man remembered

---

50. See Gavin, *"They are like the angels in the heavens."*

51. *Confessions*, XII.11.12 (Boulding, 318). Elsewhere, however (in *De Genesi ad Litteram*, 4.22.39), St. Augustine seems to accept the ability of angels to self-reflection, an ability that would suggest an act of consciousness. I am thankful to Matthew Clemente for bringing this point to my attention. Kierkegaard too sees angels as without time and without history: "Even if Michael had made a record of all the errands he had been sent on and performed, this is nevertheless not his history" (*Concept of Anxiety*, 49). For Kierkegaard the historical is the result of sexuality (sexual differentiation) and, therefore, of sin. "A perfect spirit cannot be conceived as sexually qualified. This is also in accord with the teachings of the Church about the nature of the Resurrection [alluding to Matt 22:30], in accord with its representation of angles, and in accord with the dogmatic definitions with respect to the person of Christ" (*Concept of Anxiety*, 79).

52. Zizioulas, "Ἐσχατολογία καὶ Ὕπαρξη," 46. The argument is made on the basis of a passage from St Maximus's *Questiones et Dubia* 13 (PG 90:796BC).

the poor Lazarus and the relatives he had left behind. When Metropolitan John writes in the same article that "the dead are not separated from the relations that determined their historical existence, on the contrary, it is those relations that will ultimately judge their eternal future,"[53] he seems to entertain the eschatological existence of memory; otherwise, of what good would those relations be if one does not remember them? I would argue that we will remember even what is now, *sub specie temporis*, perceived as "evil"—but it will be remembered not *as* evil, for through the perspective of time that the eschaton will afford us, indeed through the perspective of the end of times, what was previously experienced as evil will be then seen with a different understanding. As Augustine observes about the heavenly city, "it will have no memory of faults or punishments."[54] I bring as an example the Lord's passion, which, when it happened, was undoubtedly perceived as the ultimate evil. Yet, that same event is now commemorated in the Eucharist, which is the prefiguration of our eschatological understanding, as the source of our salvation. The same event is presented quite differently "at the moment" and through the distance that time affords us. Finally, if the Eucharist is a foreshadowing of the eschaton so much so that what is still future (historically) can be remembered as having taken place already—that is, if the future can be evoked in the present as past—then are we not allowed to assume that in the eschatological future the past also could be evoked as present? I would suggest that a distinction between two kinds of memory is needed here, such as the one introduced by Augustine at the end of *De Civitate Dei*:

> There are, then, two kinds of knowledge of evils, one by virtue of which they are not hidden from the mind's grasp, another by virtue of which they are ingrained in felt experience. Indeed, all the vices are known in one way through the teachings of wisdom, and in quite another through the wicked life of the fool. Similarly, there are two ways of forgetting evils. The person who has education and learning forgets them in one way, the person who has actually experienced and suffered them forgets them in another way—the former when he disregards his knowledge, the latter when he is no longer in misery. It is according to this second kind of forgetting that the saints will have no memory of past evils. For they will now

---

53. Zizioulas, "Εσχατολογία καὶ Ὕπαρξη," 69.
54. Augustine, *City of God*, XXII.30 (Babcock, 553).

be free from all evils, and they will be completely erased from their feeling.⁵⁵

With or without memory, humanity cannot exist outside temporality: the distinction that Metropolitan John introduces in that same study on eschatology, a distinction between two eternities and between two times, is very useful.⁵⁶ The eternity of man, who as a creature has had a beginning, is not the same as the ageless and motionless eternity of God. The former will be enjoyed by grace, but not on the expense of the creaturely character of the creation. The beginning of creation gave to everything that is created the *permanent* characteristic of motion. "For everything that comes into existence is subject to movement," St. Maximus reminds us.⁵⁷ Surely, that movement will eschatologically come to rest in God, yet God's infinity as well as the soul's natural definition by motion allows St. Maximus to speak of a rest that is ever-moving (στάσις ἀεικίνητος).⁵⁸ The two understandings of motion that are here implied can be said to correspond to the two distinct experiences of time: one during history that is characterized by distance (διάστημα), the other at the eschaton, *epectatic* but perhaps not *diastematic* (to use these two concepts of St. Gregory of Nyssa). The former separates and divides, the latter re-collects and unites. The perceptive reader would perhaps recognize in the distinction between these two experiences of temporality an analogy to Maximus's theology of two Wills. St. Maximus dedicates a large section of his first *Theological Opusculum* (to the priest Marinus) to the eschatological destiny of the Will. There he makes quite clear that the *gnomic* Will will be retained, for he emphatically maintains that in God's kingdom there will be no identity either of God's Will itself with that of the saints or, in fact, of the Will of the saints itself with each other, but only a convergence of what they will be willing:

> Not every human's Will will be one [μία] with respect to the mode of its motion [τρόπῳ τῷ κατὰ τὴν κίνησιν]. And at no point will the Will of God and that of the saints become one in all its aspects [κατὰ πάντα τρόπον], as it seemed to some, even though the objective of God's Will [τὸ θεληθέν] and that of the saints is one, namely

---

55. Ibid.
56. Zizioulas, "Ἐσχατολογία καὶ Ὕπαρξη," 62–66.
57. Maximus, *Ambiguum 7*, PG 91:1073B; *On the Cosmic Mystery*, 50.
58. Maximus, *Ambiguum 67*, PG 91:1401A; *Questiones ad Thalasium 65*, PG 90:760A; *Capita de Caritate*, 3, 25, PG 90:1024C. See Sherwood, *Earlier Ambigua*, 194 n. 24, and also Betsakos's study Στάσις Ἀεικίνητος.

the salvation of the elect, that being a divine goal and an end preconceived before all ages, and a point about which the Will of the saints among themselves and the Will of the God who saves them will converge [γενήσεται σύμβασις].... For God's Will desires by its nature the salvation of men, while, on the other hand, humanity wills by nature its salvation; thus, that which saves and that which is saved can never be the same [ταυτὸν], even if the goal of both is everyone's salvation, as proposed by God and chosen by men.[59]

Then, St. Maximus goes on to argue *ad absurdum* what would have been the untenable conclusions that we would be forced to draw if we were to entertain such an identity between the Wills of the saints or their Will and that of God. It seems that for St. Maximus our two Wills will retain their integrity in the age to come as much as in the present age, or better yet, even more then, when the discord between them will have been brought to harmony with each other and immutability (ἀτρεψία) with regard to their object of desire.

In the mature articulation on the subject that *Opusculum 3* represents, St. Maximus differentiates between the two Wills by defining natural Will only as a possibility, as an ability that is actualized (after an Aristotelian fashion) by a particular some-one, a willing one (ὁ θέλων). In order to elucidate his distinction, St. Maximus provides an example, that of language:

> To be disposed by nature to will and to will are not the same thing, as it is not the same thing to be disposed by nature to speak and to speak. For the capacity for speaking is always naturally there, but one does not always speak, since what belongs to the essence is contained in the principle of the nature, while what belongs to the wish is shaped by the intention [*gnōmē*] of the one who speaks. So being able to speak always belongs to the nature, but *how* you speak belongs to the *hypostasis*. So it is with being disposed by nature to will and willing.[60]

Even if, at the end of times, we all will say the same thing, namely "your will be done," as we all say now the "Amen" in the liturgical prefiguration of the *eschaton*, that unison does not obliterate difference, for "how you speak belongs to the hypostasis"; thus we are allowed to utter our prayers and our "amens" not only in our languages and idioms, but also with our distinct

---

59. Maximus, *Opusculum 1*, PG 91:25AB, my translation.

60. Maximus, *Opusculum 3*, PG 91:43A, translation in Louth, *Maximus the Confessor*, 193.

accents. Will, like language—to continue borrowing from St. Maximus's example—is highly idiomatic as much as it is hypostatic. No one doubts that the capacity to speak is endowed by nature—yet, paradoxically, a nature that is not enhypostasized in the human person is mute. Neither the "your will be done" of the Lord's Prayer nor the "*maranatha*" of the Church is or can be uttered by nature. In the great conversation between God and humanity that began with the world's creation and will continue in the *epektasis* of "the ages of ages," only persons can be partakers.

Bibliography

Afanassieff, Nicholas. "The Church Which Presides in Love." In *The Primacy of Peter*, edited by John Meyendorff, 91–143. Crestwood: St. Vladimir's Seminary Press, 1992.
Androutsos, Christos. Δογματική. Athens: Τυπογραφεῖον τοῦ Κράτους, 1907.
Arendt, Hannah. *The Life of the Mind*. 2 vols. New York: Harcourt Brace Jovanovich, 1978.
Augustine. Περὶ Τριάδος. Translated by Maximos Planudes. Athens: Academy of Athens, 1995.
———. *The City of God (De Civitate Dei)*. Translated by William Babcock. New York: New City, 2012.
———. *Confessions*. Translated by Maria Boulding. New York: New City, 1997.
———. *Earlier Writings*. Translated by John H. S. Burleigh. Library of Christian Classics 6. Philadelphia: Westminster, 1953.
———. *Expositions of the Psalms*. Translated by Maria Boulding. Edited by John E. Rotelle. New York: New City Press, 2002.
———. *Letters (Epistulae)*. Vol. 2, *Letters, 100–155*. Translated by Roland Teske. Edited by John E. Rotelle. New York: New City, 2003.
———. *The Literal Meaning of Genesis (De Genesi ad Litteram)*. In *On Genesis*. Translated by Edmund Hill. Edited by John E. Rotelle. New York: New City, 2002.
———. *Miscellany of Questions in Response to Simplician I*. In *Selected Writings on Grace and Pelagianism*. Translated by Roland Teske. New York: New City Press, 2011.
———. *The Trinity (De Trinitate)*. Translated by Edmund Hill. Edited by John E. Rotelle. New York: New City, 1991.
Balthasar, Hans Urs von. *Cosmic Liturgy: The Universe According to Maximus the Confessor*. Translated by Brian E. Daley. San Francisco: Ignatius, 1988.
———. *The Glory of the Lord*. 7 vols. Transaled by Erasmo Leiva-Merikakis et al. San Francisco: Ignatius, 1983–.
———. *The Office of Peter and the Structure of the Church*. Translated by Andrée Emery. San Francisco: Ignatius, 1986.
———. *Theo-Logic*. Vol. 3, *The Spirit of Truth*. Translated by Graham Harrison. San Francisco: Ignatius, 2005.
Barnes, Michel René. "The Visible Christ and the Invisible Trinity: Mt 5:8 in Augustine's Trinitarian Theology of 400." *Modern Theology* 19 (2003) 329–56.
Bartholomew, Ecumenical Patriarch. Address by His All-Holiness Ecumenical Patriarch Bartholomew to His Holiness Pope Francis during the Divine Liturgy for the Feast of St. Andrew. November 30, 2014. http://www.patriarchate.org/-/address-by-his-all-

Bibliography

holiness-ecumenical-patriarch-bartholomew-to-his-holiness-pope-francis-during-the-divine-liturgy-for-the-feast-of-st-andrew-in-the-.

Bartholomew, Ecumenical Patriarch, and Pope Francis. Joint Declaration of the Apostolic Pilgrimage in Jerusalem. May 25, 2014. http://www.apostolicpilgrimage.org/joint-declaration.

Berthold, George C. "Did Maximus the Confessor Know Augustine?" *Studia Patristica* 17 (1982) 14–17.

Betsakos, Vasileios. Στάσις Ἀεικίνητος. Athens: Armos, 2006.

Bond, H. Lawrence. "From Constantinople to 'Learned Ignorance': The Historical Matrix for the Formation of the *De docta ignorantia*." In *Nicholas of Cusa on Christ and the Church*, edited by Gerald Christianson and Thomas M. Izbicki, 135–65. Leiden: Brill, 1996.

Bulgakov, Sergius. *The Comforter*. Translated by Boris Jakim. Grand Rapids: Eerdmans, 2004.

Cassidy, Edward Idris. *Ecumenism and Interreligious Dialogue*. New York: Paulist, 2005.

Chesterton, G. K. "Mr. Bernard Shaw." In vol. 1 of *G. K. Chesterton's Collected Works*. San Francisco: Ignatius, 1986.

———. Orthodoxy. In vol. 1 of *G. K. Chesterton's Collected Works*. San Francisco: Ignatius, 1986.

Chryssavgis, John, ed. *Dialogue of Love: Breaking the Silence of Centuries*. New York: Fordham University Press, 2014.

Clapsis, Emmanuel. "The Papal Primacy." *Greek Orthodox Theological Review* 32 (1987) 115–30.

Congar, Yves. *I Believe in the Holy Spirit*. 3 vols in 1. New York: Herder & Herder, 2005.

Constas, Nicholas. "An Apology for the Cult of Saints in Late Antiquity: Eustratius Presbyter of Constantinople, *On the State of Souls after Death* (CPG 7522)." *Journal of Early Christian Studies* 10 (2002) 267–85.

Cyril of Alexandria. *In Joannis Evangelium*. In Patrologia graeca 74. Edited by J.-P. Migne. 162 vols. Paris, 1857–1886.

Daley, Brian. "Introduction." In *On the Dormition of Mary: Early Patristic Homilies*, translated by Brian Daley, 1–45. Crestwood: St. Vladimir's Seminary Press, 1997.

———. "Making a Human Will Divine: Augustine and Maximus on Christ and Human Salvation." In *Orthodox Readings of Augustine*, edited by George Demacopoulos and Aristotle Papanikolaou, 101–26. Crestwood, NY: St. Vladimir's Seminary Press, 2008.

———. "Position and Patronage in the Early Church." *Journal of Theological Studies* 44 (1993) 529–53.

Demacopoulos, George, and Aristotle Papanikolaou. "Augustine and the Orthodox: The West in the East." In *Orthodox Readings of Augustine*, edited by George Demacopoulos and Aristotle Papanikolaou, 11–40. Crestwood, NY: St. Vladimir's Seminary Press, 2008.

———, eds. *Orthodox Readings of Augustine*. Crestwood, NY: St. Vladimir's Seminary Press, 2008.

Demetrakopoulos, Andronikos. *Bibliotheca Ecclesiastica*. Hildesheim: Georg Olms, 1965.

Descartes, René. *Meditations on First Philosophy*. In vol. 2 of *The Philosophical Writings of Descartes*. Translated by John Cottingham et al. Cambridge: Cambridge University Press, 1984.

Bibliography

DeVille, Adam A. J. *Orthodoxy and the Roman Papacy.* Notre Dame: University of Notre Dame Press, 2011.

Eustratius. *De Statu Animarum Post Mortem.* Edited by Peter Van Deun. Corpus Christianorum series Graeca 60. Turnhout: Brepols, 2006.

Farrow, Douglas. *Ascension and Ecclesia: On the Significance of the Doctrine of the Ascension for Ecclesiology and Christian Cosmology.* Grand Rapids: Eerdmans, 1999.

Flogaus, Reinhard. "Inspiration-Exploitation-Distortion: The Use of St Augustine in the Hesychast Controversy." In *Orthodox Readings of Augustine,* edited by George Demacopoulos and Aristotle Papanikolaou, 63–80. Crestwood, NY: St. Vladimir's Seminary Press, 2008.

———. "Palamas and Barlaam Revisited: A Reassessment of East and West in the Hesychast Controversy of 14th Century Byzantium." In *St. Vladimir's Theological Quarterly* 42 (1998) 1–32.

Florensky, Pavel. *The Pillar and Ground of the Truth.* Translated by Boris Jakim. Princeton: Princeton University Press, 1997.

Francis, Pope. Address at the Ecumenical Celebration on the Occasion of the Fiftieth Anniversary of the Meeting between Pope Paul VI and Patriarch Athenagoras in Jerusalem. May 25, 2014. http://w2.vatican.va/content/francesco/en/speeches/2014/may/documents/papa-francesco_20140525_terra-santa-celebrazione-ecumenica.html.

———. Address by His Holiness Pope Francis to His All-Holiness Ecumenical Patriarch Bartholomew during the Doxology in the Patriarchal Church. November 29, 2014. http://www.patriarchate.org/-/address-by-his-holiness-pope-francis-to-his-all-holiness-ecumenical-patriarch-bartholomew-during-the-doxology-in-the-patriarchal-church-november-29-20.

Garrigues, Jean-Miguel. *L'Esprit qui dit "Père!": L'Esprit-Saint dans la vie trinitaire et le problème du Filioque.* Paris: Téqui, 1981.

Gavin, John. *"They are like the angels in the heavens": Angelology and Anthropology in the Thought of Maximus the Confessor.* Rome: Institutum Patristicum Augustinianum, 2009.

Gregory Nazianzen. *Die fünf theologischen Reden.* Edited by Joseph Barbel. Düsseldorf: Patmos, 1963.

———. *Oration 38 (On Theophany).* In Patrologia graeca 36. Edited by J.-P. Migne. 162 vols. Paris, 1857–86.

Gregory Palamas. Συγγράμματα. Edited by Panagiotis Christou. 5 vols. Thessalonica, 1988.

Hart, Kevin, ed. *Counter-Experiences: Reading Jean-Luc Marion.* Notre Dame: University of Notre Dame, 2007.

Husserl, Edmund. *Logical Investigations.* Translated by J. N. Findlay. New York: Humanities, 1970.

Ioannides, Nikolaos. Ο Ἰωσὴφ Βρυέννιος: Βίος-Ἔργα-Διδασκαλία [Josef Bryennios: Life, Work, Teaching]. Athens, 1996.

Irenaeus. *Against Heresies.* Translated and edited by Alexander Roberts and James Donaldson. In vol. 1 of *Ante-Nicene Fathers.* Peabody, MA: Hedrickson, 2004.

Jevtić, Atanasije. Χριστός: Ἀρχὴ καὶ Τέλος. Athens: Goulandri-Horn, 1983.

John of Damascus. *Die Schriften des Johannes von Damaskos.* Edited by Bonifatius Kotter. Patristische Texte und Studien 29. Berlin de Gruyter, 1988.

Bibliography

Joint International Commission for the Theological Dialogue between the Roman Catholic Church and the Orthodox Church. "Ecclesiological and Canonical Consequences of the Sacramental Nature of the Church: Ecclesial Communion, Conciliarity and Authority" (The Ravenna Statement). *Pontifical Council for Promoting Christian Unity Information Service*, no. 126, 2007.

Jugie, Martin. *L'Immaculée Conception dans l'Écriture Sainte et dans la tradition oriental.* Rome: Officium Libri Catholici, 1952.

Kappes, Christiaan W. *The Immaculate Conception.* New Bedford, MA: Academy of the Immaculate, 2014.

Kearney, Richard. *Strangers, Gods, and Monsters: Interpreting Otherness.* London: Routledge, 2002.

Kierkegaard, Søren. *The Concept of Anxiety.* Translated by Reidar Thomte. Princeton: Princeton University Press, 1980.

Kimball, Virginia M. *Liturgical Illuminations: Discovering Received Tradition in the Eastern Orthros of Feasts of the Theotokos.* Bloomington: AuthorHouse, 2010.

Kloos, Kari. "Preparing for the Vision of God: Augustine's Interpretation of the Biblical Theophany Narratives." *Augustinian Studies* 36 (2005) 394–420.

Lambriniadis, Elpidophoros. "Challenges of Orthodoxy in America and the Role of the Ecumenical Patriarchate." Speech delivered at the Chapel of the Holy Cross, Greek Orthodox School of Theology, Brookline, Massachusetts, March 18, 2009. http://www.ecclesia.gr/englishnews/default.asp?id=3986.

———. "First Without Equals: A Response to the Text on Primacy of the Moscow Patriarchate." http://www.patriarchate.org/theological-and-other-studies/-/asset_publisher/GovONi6kIiut/content/primus-sine-paribus-hapantesis-eis-to-peri-proteiou-keimenon-tou-patriarcheiou-moschas-tou-sebasmiotatou-metropolitou-prouses-k-elpidophorou?languageId=en_US.

Léthel, François-Marie. *Théologie de l'agonie du Christ.* Paris: Beauchesne, 1979.

Levinas, Emmanuel. *Existence and Existents.* Translated by Alphonso Lingis. The Hague: Martinus Nijhoff, 1978.

Lossky, Vladimir. *The Mystical Theology of the Eastern Church.* Translated by members of the Fellowship of St. Alban and St. Sergius. Crestwood, NY: St. Vladimir's Seminary Press, 1976.

Louth, Andrew. *Greek East and Latin West: The Church, A.D. 681–1071.* The Church in History 3. Crestwood, NY: St. Vladimir's Seminary Press, 2007.

———. *Maximus the Confessor.* London: Routledge, 1996.

Macquarrie, John. *Jesus Christ in Modern Thought.* London: SCM, 1990.

Manoussakis, John Panteleimon. "The Anarchic Principle of Christian Eschatology in the Eucharistic Tradition of the Eastern Church." *Harvard Theological Review* 100 (2007) 27–46.

———. *God After Metaphysics: A Theological Aesthetic.* Bloomington: Indiana University Press, 2007.

———. "Primacy and Ecclesiology: The State of the Question." In *Orthodox Constructions of the West*, edited by Aristotle Papanikolaou and George Demacopoulos, 229–39. New York: Fordham University Press, 2013.

———. "Thebes Revisited: Theodicy and the Temporality of Ethics." *Research in Phenomenology* 39 (2009) 292–306.

———. "Theophany and Indication: Reconciling Augustinian and Palamite Aesthetics." *Modern Theology* 26 (2010) 79–92.

Bibliography

Maximus the Confessor. *Disputatio cum Pyrrho*. In Patrologia graeca 91. Edited by J.-P. Migne. 162 vols. Paris, 1857–1886.

———. *Epistolae*. In Patrologia graeca 91. Edited by J.-P. Migne. 162 vols. Paris, 1857–1886.

———. *Expositio Orationis Dominicae*. In Patrologia graeca 90. Edited by J.-P. Migne. 162 vols. Paris, 1857–1886.

———. *On the Cosmic Mystery of Jesus Christ*. Translated by Paul M. Blowers and Robert Louis Wilken. Crestwood, NY: St. Vladimir's Seminary Press, 2003.

———. *On Difficulties in the Church Fathers: The Ambigua*. Edited and translated by Nicholas Constas. 2 vols. Dumbarton Oaks Medieval Library 28–29. Cambridge: Harvard University Press, 2014.

———. *Opuscula Theologica et Polemica*. In Patrologia graeca 91. Edited by J.-P. Migne. 162 vols. Paris, 1857–1886.

———. *Questiones ad Thalassium*. In Patrologia graeca 90. Edited by J.-P. Migne. 162 vols. Paris, 1857–1886.

———. *Questiones et Dubia*. In Patrologia graeca 91. Edited by J.-P. Migne. 162 vols. Paris, 1857–1886.

McFarland, Ian A. "'Naturally and by Grace': Maximus the Confessor on the Operation of the Will." *Scottish Journal of Theology* 58 (2005) 410–33.

McPartlan, Paul. *A Service of Love: Papal Primacy, the Eucharist and Church Unity*. Washington, DC: Catholic University of America Press, 2013.

Merleau-Ponty, Maurice. *The Visible and the Invisible*. Translated by Alphonso Lingis. Evanston: Northwestern University Press, 1968.

Murray, Michael J. "Introduction." In G. W. Leibniz, *Dissertation on Predestination and Grace*, translated and edited by Michael J. Murray, xv–li. New Haven: Yale University Press, 2011.

Nicholas of Cusa. *Writings on Church and Reform*. Translated by Thomas M. Izbicki. I Tatti Renaissance Library 33. Cambridge: Harvard University Press, 2008.

Nichols, Aidan. *Rome and the Eastern Churches*. 2nd ed. San Francisco: Ignatius, 2010.

Oeldemann, Johannes. *Orthodoxe Kirchen im Ökumenischen Dialog: Positionen, Probleme, Perspektiven*. Paderbon: Bonifatius, 2004.

Origen. *Homilies on Luke*. Translated by Joseph T. Lienhard. Washington, DC: Catholic University of America Press, 1996.

Papadakis, Aristeides. *The Christian East and the Rise of the Papacy: The Church, A.D. 1071–1453*. The Church in History 4. Crestwood, NY: St. Vladimir's Seminary Press, 1994.

Pelikan, Jaroslav. *Mary Through the Centuries*. New Haven: Yale University Press, 1996.

Photius of Constantinople. *De Spiritus Sancti Mystagogia*. In Patrologia graeca 102. Edited by J.-P. Migne. 162 vols. Paris, 1857–1886.

———. *Homilia I: In Sanctae Mariae Nativitatem*. In Patrologia graeca 102. Edited by J.-P. Migne. 162 vols. Paris, 1857–1886.

Plested, Marcus. *Orthodox Readings of Aquinas*. Oxford: Oxford University Press, 2012.

Rahner, Karl. *Theological Investigations*. Vol. 4, *More Recent Writings*. London: Darton, Longman & Todd, 1966.

Ratzinger, Joseph. *Eschatology: Death and Eternal Life*. Translated by Michael Waldstein. 2nd ed. Washington, DC: Catholic University of America Press, 1988.

Bibliography

Second Vatican Council. *Unitatis Redintegratio*. http://www.vatican.va/archive/hist_councils/ii_vatican_council/documents/vat-ii_decree_19641121_unitatis-redintegratio_en.html.

Sherwood, Polycarp. *The Earlier Ambigua of Saint Maximus the Confessor and his Refutation of Origenism*. Rome: Pontificium Institutum S. Anselmi, 1955.

Sophronius of Jerusalem. *Oratio II: Ad Annuntiationem*. In Patrologia graeca 87/3. Edited by J.-P. Migne. 162 vols. Paris, 1857–1886.

Sorabji, Richard. "The Concept of the Will from Plato to Maximus the Confessor." In *The Will and Human Action*, edited by Thomas Pink and M. W. F. Stone, 6–28. London: Routledge, 2004.

Spourlakou-Eutychiadou, Amalia. "The Most Holy Theotokos as a Model of Christian Sanctity." PhD diss., National University of Athens, 1990.

Stylianopoulos, Theodore. "The *Filioque*: Dogma, Theologoumenon or Error?" In *Spirit of Truth: Ecumenical Perspective on the Holy Spirit*, edited by Theodore Stylianopoulos and S. Mark Heim, 25–58. Brookline, MA: Holy Cross Orthodox Press, 1986.

Taft, Robert. "Perceptions and Realities in Orthodox-Catholic Relations Today: Reflections on the Past, Prospects for the Future." In *Orthodox Constructions of the West*, edited by G. Demacopoulos and A. Papanikolaou, 23–44. New York: Fordham University Press, 2013.

Theodore the Studite. *Letter 33*. In Patrologia graeca 99. Edited by J.-P. Migne. 162 vols. Paris, 1857–1886.

Thunberg, Lars. *Microcosm and Mediator: The Theological Anthropology of Maximus the Confessor*. Chicago: Open Court, 1995.

Trempelas, Panayiotis. Δογματική τῆς Ὀρθοδόξου Καθολικῆς Ἐκκλησίας. Athens: ΣΩΤΗΡ, 1979.

Vgenopoulos, Maximos. *Primacy in the Church from Vatican I to Vatican II: An Orthodox Perspective*. DeKalb: Northern Illinois University Press, 2013.

Vischer, Lukas, ed. *Spirit of God, Spirit of Christ: Ecumenical Reflection on the Filioque Controversy*. Geneva: WCC, 1981.

Ware, Kallistos (Timothy). "The Transfiguration of the Body." In *Sacrament and Image: Essays in the Christian Understanding of Man*, edited by A. M Allchin, 17–32. London: Fellowship of S. Alban and S. Sergius, 1967.

Watts, Thomas A. "Two Wills in Christ?" *Westminster Theological Journal* 71 (2009) 455–87.

Zizioulas, John. *Being as Communion*. Crestwood, NY: St. Vladimir's Seminary Press, 1985.

———. *Communion and Otherness*. Edited by Paul McPartlan. London: T. & T. Clark, 2006.

———. *Eucharist, Bishop, Church: The Unity of the Church in the Divine Eucharist and the Bishop during the Three First Centuries*. Translated by Elizabeth Theokritoff. Brookline, MA: Holy Cross Orthodox Press, 2001.

———. "Person and Nature in the Theology of St Maximus the Confessor." In *Knowing the Purpose of Creation through the Resurrection*, edited by Bishop Maxim (Vasiljević), 85–143. Los Angeles: Sebastian, 2013.

———. "Recent Discussions on Primacy in Orthodox Theology." In *The Petrine Ministry: Catholics and Orthodox in Dialogue*, edited by Walter Kasper, 231–48. New York: Newman, 2006.

Bibliography

———. "Ἐσχατολογία καὶ Ὕπαρξη: Μιὰ ὀντολογικὴ προσέγγιση στὸ πρόβλημα τῶν ἐσχάτων." Σύναξη 121 (2012) 43–72.

———. "Ἡ Εὐχαριστιακὴ Ἐκκλησιολογία στὴν Ὀρθόδοξη Παράδοση." Θεολογία 80 (2009) 5–25.

———. "Ὁ Συνοδικὸς Θεσμός: Ἱστορικά, Ἐκκλησιολογικὰ καὶ Κανονικὰ Προβλήματα." Θεολογία 80 (2009) 5–41.

Index

Afanassieff, Nicholas, 29, 31–32
Aquinas, Thomas. *See* Thomas Aquinas.
Arendt, Hannah, 69, 80
Athenagoras, Ecumenical Patriarch, xviii
Augustine of Hippo, xv–xvii, 14, 17, 19–20, 51–53, 55–58, 60, 65–70, 73, 76–78, 80–82, 87, 88

Balthasar, Hans Urs von, 17, 19, 24, 51, 59, 64, 68, 78, 80, 82–83
Barnes, Michel René, 55
Bartholomew, Ecumenical Patriarch, xv, xviii, xix, 37, 39, 46
Benedict XVI. *See* Ratziner, Joseph.
Bond, Lawrence, xvi
Bulgakov, Sergius, 17

Cassidy, Edward Idris, 28–29, 45, 48
Chesterton, G. K., 38, 43
Chryssavgis, John, xviii
Clapsis, Emmanuel, 24
Congar, Yves, 15, 17, 44
Constantinople, 2, 36, 39–43
Constas, Nicholas, 57, 80
Cusanus. *See* Nicholas of Cusa.
Cyril of Alexandria, 8
Cyril of Jerusalem, 34

Daley, Brian, 6, 38, 39, 77
Demacopoulos, George, xv, xvi, 52
Descartes, René, 74–75
Duns Scotus, 12

Eschatology (eschaton), xvii, 12, 13, 64, 67, 82, 87–90
Eugene IV, Pope, xv
Eustratius, 57, 62

Farrow, Douglas, 31
Filioque, xvii, 15–19, 21, 26
Flogaus, Reinhard, 52
Florensky, Pavel, 26
Francis, Pope, xviii, xix, 39, 45, 46

Garrigues, Jean-Miguel, 15, 18–20
Gregory of Nyssa, 89
Gregory of Thessalonica (Palamas), xvi, xvii, 20, 52–53, 57, 61–62, 66–67
Gregory, Nazianzen, 10, 16, 23, 34
Gregory, Zigavinos, 24

Hart, Kevin, 60
Heidegger, Martin, 81, 86

Ignatius of Antioch, 30
Irenaeus of Lyon, 9–10, 54

John of Damascus, 10, 11
John Paul II, Pope, 15, 39
Jugie, Martin 8

Kappes, Christiaan W., 5, 10,
Kearney, Richard, 26
Kierkegaard, Søren, 73, 86–87
Kimbal, Virginia, 6
Kydones, Demetrios, 1

Index

Lambriniadis, Elpidophoros, 27–28, 33–34, 35, 42
Leibniz, Gottfried Wilhelm von, xv, xvi
Leo III, Pope, 15
Leo, Pope, 28, 35
Levinas, Emmanuel, 85–86
Lossky, Vladimir, 34, 61
Louth, Andrew 2, 9, 70, 77, 84, 90

Martin V, Pope, xv
Maximus the Confessor, xvii, 17, 69–71, 74–81, 83–87, 89–91
McPartlan, Paul, 24, 30–31, 35, 38
Merleau-Ponty, Maurice, 59
Michael of Constantinople (Cerularios), 8

Neopalamites, 61
Nicholas of Cusa (Cusanus), xv, 23–25, 28, 40
Nichols, Aidan, 15–16, 18–19, 21, 23, 27, 36, 38, 40

Oeldemann, Johannes, 2
Origen, 7, 8, 53, 78, 79

Palamas. *See* Gregory of Thessalonica.
Papadakis, Aristeides, 22, 27
Papanikolaou, Aristotle, xv, xvi, 52
Pelikan, Jaroslav, 6, 12,
Photius of Constantinople, 10, 12, 17, 52

Planudes, Maximos 20, 52
Plested, Marcus xvii, 1, 21
Primus, 5, 22–23, 25, 26–31, 33, 37–38, 47

Rahner, Karl 17, 44
Ratzinger, Joseph (Pope Benedict XVI), xv, 15, 39
Ravenna Statement, 24, 27, 31, 40, 48
Rome, 2, 22, 24, 26–27, 28, 36, 39–41, 47

Schism, xvi, 1–2, 22, 26, 41
Schmemann, Alexander, 29, 47
Sherwood, Polycarp, 79, 81, 89
Sophronius of Jerusalem, 9, 12
Sorabji, Richard, 69
Stylianopoulos, Theodore, 16

Taft, Robert, xiv
Theodore the Studite, 35–36
Thomas Aquinas, xvi–xvii, 21, 72

Vgenopoulos, Maximos, 24, 29, 31–32, 35, 38, 47–48

Ware, Kallistos (Timothy), 67

Zizioulas, John D., 16, 25, 28–31, 33–35, 38, 47, 61, 71, 79, 82–83, 87, 88, 89

www.ingramcontent.com/pod-product-compliance
Lightning Source LLC
Chambersburg PA
CBHW032233080426
42735CB00008B/841